# Theos Friends' Programme

Theos is a religion and society think tank which seeks to inform opinion about the role of faith and belief in society.

We were launched in November 2006 with the support of Dr Rowan Williams and the Cardinal Archbishop of Westminster, Cardinal Cormac Murphy-O'Connor.

## We provide

- high-quality research, reports and publications;
- an events programme;
- news, information and analysis to media companies, parliamentarians and other opinion formers.

## We can only do this with your help!

Theos Friends receive complimentary copies of all Theos publications, invitations to selected events and monthly email bulletins.

Theos Associates receive all the benefits of Friends and in addition are invited to attend an exclusive annual dinner with the Theos Director and team.

If you would like to become a Friend or an Associate, please visit www.theosthinktank.co.uk or detach or photocopy the form below, and send it with a cheque to Theos for the relevant amount. Thank you.

---

Yes, I would like to help change public opinion!
I enclose a cheque payable to Theos for:  ☐ **£60** (Friend)   ☐ **£300** (Associate)

☐ Please send me information on how to give by standing order/direct debit

Name _____

Address _____

_____ Postcode _____

Email _____

Tel _____

**Data Protection** Theos will use your personal data to inform you of its activities.
If you prefer not to receive this information please tick here. ☐

*By completing you are consenting to receiving communications by telephone and email. Theos will not pass on your details to any third party.*

*Please return this form to:*
Theos | 77 Great Peter Street | London | SW1P 2EZ
S: 97711 D: 36701

**Theos**

# Theos

## Theos – clear thinking on religion and society

Theos is a Christian think tank working in the area of religion, politics and society. We aim to inform debate around questions of faith and secularism and the related subjects of values and identity. We were launched in November 2006, and our first report *'Doing God': a Future for Faith in the Public Square,* written by Nick Spencer, examined the reasons why faith will play an increasingly significant role in public life.

## what Theos stands for

In our post-secular age, interest in spirituality is increasing across western culture. We believe that it is impossible to understand the modern world without an understanding of religion. We also believe that much of the debate about the role and place of religion has been unnecessarily emotive and ill-informed. We reject the notion of any possible 'neutral' perspective on these issues.

## what Theos works on

Theos conducts research, publishes reports and runs debates, seminars and lectures on the intersection of religion, politics and society in the contemporary world. We also provide regular comment for print and broadcast media. Research areas include religion in relation to public services, the constitution, law, the economy, pluralism and education.

## what Theos provides

In addition to our independently driven work, Theos provides research, analysis and advice to individuals and organisations across the private, public and not-for-profit sectors. Our unique position within the think tank sector means that we have the capacity to develop proposals that carry values – with an eye to demonstrating what really works.

## what Theos believes

Theos was launched with the support of the Archbishop of Canterbury and the Cardinal Archbishop of Westminster, but it is independent of any particular denomination. We are an ecumenical Christian organisation, committed to the belief that religion in general and Christianity in particular has much to offer for the common good of society as a whole. We are committed to the traditional creeds of the Christian faith and draw on social and political thought from a wide range of theological traditions. We also work with many non-Christian and non-religious individuals and organisations.

# The Case for Christian Humanism:

## Why Christians should believe in humanism, and humanists in Christianity

Angus Ritchie and Nick Spencer

Foreword by Rowan Williams

## Acknowledgement

We are grateful to the New Insights & Directions for Religious Epistemology research project (newinsights.ox.ac.uk) at Oxford University for funding this report, and public debates on its content, as part of its dissemination and engagement work. The New Insights project has been made possible through a generous grant from the John Templeton Foundation. We are also grateful to Hymns Ancient and Modern for their grant towards the production of this report and subsequent events discussing its arguments.

Published by Theos in 2014
© Theos

ISBN 978-0-9574743-6-9

Some rights reserved – see copyright licence for details
For further information and subscription details please contact:

Theos
Licence Department
77 Great Peter Street
London
SW1P 2EZ

T 020 7828 7777
E hello@theosthinktank.co.uk
www.theosthinktank.co.uk

# contents

| | | |
|---|---|---|
| foreword | | 6 |
| introduction | | 9 |
| chapter 1 | – being generous with humanism | 14 |
| chapter 2 | – why reason? | 31 |
| chapter 3 | – why dignity? | 44 |
| chapter 4 | – why morality? | 61 |

# foreword

Christians believe that what they speak of and try to live by is a truth that brings 'abundance' to human life: "I have come that they may have life, and have it to the full" (John 10.10).

That is the charter for speaking of a Christian 'humanism', a tradition that goes right back to the days of earliest Christianity, where we find the second century writer Irenaeus of Lyons saying that "the glory of God is a human being fully alive", and is echoed by some of the great Christian minds of the twentieth century such as the Roman Catholic Jacques Maritain and the Anglican Michael Ramsey.

Archbishop Ramsey wrote, in a book review of the late 1960s, that

> Europe knew a long tradition of avowedly Christian humanism drawn from the confluence of the stream of biblical theism from Palestine and the stream of classical humanism from ancient Greece'.[1]

In the same essay he invited Christians to rediscover that tradition, confident that "no truth is to be feared since all truth is of God."[2] The idea that human flourishing had to entail the decline of religion needed – and still needs – demythologising. But that will only happen if we can inject some clarity into what is often a sterile debate between Christians and secular humanists.

There are those on the one side who argue fiercely that concessions to a 'humanist' mindset weaken the radical challenge of the gospel to all human arrogance and self-sufficiency. Surely faith begins when human confidence bows before the alien majesty of God and recognises that all its achievement is valueless without the summons and gift of grace? And on the other side of the argument are those who would like to see religion classified as a clinical mental disorder and who cannot see any role at all for belief in an adult and rational universe.

To the first camp, it needs to be said that the sovereign power of grace is not in competition with human well-being and even proper human confidence. If we need grace and have to recognise ourselves as deeply estranged from God's purpose, this is because we have become estranged from the dignity that is *meant* to be ours; we need to be restored to ourselves not transformed into some *in*human purity.

To the second – apart perhaps from a reminder of what sort of human regimes in the modern age have categorised dissenters or minorities as mentally disordered – it must be said that the resourcefulness of faith in feeding human imagination and motivating resistance to various political claims to absolute power has to be acknowledged as something that has served a 'humanist' end, whatever you may think of the truth of faith's assertions.

There is, in fact, room for a good and significant conversation in our society about where exactly our convictions of human dignity or equality or liberty come from and how they are to be defended, in theory and practice. This clear and creative study shows that Michael Ramsey's challenge can be met in a way that engages vigorously with those who see faith as the enemy of human well-being; it charts a persuasive path through complex discussions and offers grounds for a reaffirmation of the bold claim that the gospel invites all into a fuller, not a narrower, human reality.

*Rowan Williams was 104th Archbishop of Canterbury and is currently Master of Magdalene College, Cambridge.*

# foreword – references

1. Michael Ramsey, 'Christ and Humanism', p. 45, in *Canterbury Pilgrim*, (London: SPCK, 1974), pp. 45-48.
2. Ibid., p.47.

# introduction

## 1.

The Christian capacity to fight over labels is legendary. For centuries Christians split from, denounced and then even persecuted other Christians who weren't quite the right kind of Christian. For a religion founded on saviour who told his first followers, "as I have loved you, so you must love one another. By this everyone will know that you are my disciples," this much rank as a tragedy beyond measure.

Religions are particularly bad at this but they do not have the monopoly on identity exclusion. That great secular religion, Marxism, was as fissiparous as any Protestant church, parsing its ideological differences in forensic detail and excluding those who did not concur with whatever interpretation of Marx's *oeuvre* was in vogue at that time. There seems to be an innate human inclination to try to own certain identities by excluding others, an inclination that, if anything, intensifies the closer people actually are to one another. The narcissism of small difference can be overpowering.

This essay is written, in part, to help guard against an important modern ideology, humanism, going the same way. In the words of the Rationalist Press Association,

> too many members of the organised Humanist movement, who call themselves Humanists and call for Humanism, are too much inclined to make the mistake of trying to appropriate these words, to claim them as being 'our own', and to restrict their use to our sense.[1]

This essay has two objectives, the first of which is to counter this spirit of 'restriction'. It argues, in the first instance, that Christianity shares much in common with humanism and that Christians (and indeed many other religious people, though its focus is on Christianity) should think of themselves as humanists. Precisely what humanism is, what beliefs and commitments it entails, and whether it is dogmatic or merely suggestive is not always clear. Chapter 1 looks at some of these definitions. 'Humanism', it argues, drawing on various humanist statements and publications, has meant a wide range of different things over the years and has long been a 'broad church', sheltering different groups that have shared but not identical commitments.

That recognised, the chapter is also clear that words do change their meaning and that just because a word might once have meant one thing, it doesn't necessarily still do so. This is technically known as the etymological fallacy – the idea that the current meaning of a word is the same as its historic meaning(s) – and it is mistake to apply it to 'humanism'.

For that reason, Chapter 1 goes on to discuss a number of recent definitions of humanism, to see how the term is understood and applied today, in particular by those who prominently call themselves 'humanist'. Of the various definitions discussed, the chapter follows the British Humanist Association in treating the 2002 Amsterdam Declaration of the International Humanist and Ethical Union as (in the BHA's words) "the fullest definition to have a measure of international agreement". This contains a great many creeds, beliefs and sentiments that many Christians will wholeheartedly share. In this way, the chapter demonstrates that the case for Christian humanism, as opposed to, say, atheistic or secular humanism, rests not simply on historical or etymological foundations but on up-to-date and authoritative definitions.

This is the first part (although only one chapter) of this essay: humanism comprises a positive (set of) creed(s) that are consonant with Christianity and worthy of Christian support. It is an argument that we hope will be relatively uncontroversial, not least as it is already articulated by atheist humanists themselves. In the words of one,

> the facts are that while *Humanism* happens to be the word we now use, it isn't 'our own'; that it has been, is being, and will be used by many other people in many other ways; that most of its senses have actually involved religion; that many of its non-religious senses are unclear without qualification; [and] that all viable senses of a word are equally valid…[2]

So far, so uncontentious. The second part of the essay will be more contestable and will be more controversial. It is, in effect, that although 'humanism' is a term that may be used by people of all kinds of religious and non-religious commitments, only belief in God can provide a sufficiently robust philosophical foundation to sustain some of its most fundamental claims.

The Amsterdam Declaration discussed in Chapter 1 outlines a range of claims, but we have chosen to focus on three of the most commonly mentioned, important and fundamental. Firstly, humanism is "rational", recognising that "reliable knowledge of the world and ourselves arises through a continuing process of observation, evaluation and revision".

Second, humanism affirms the human, being committed to the "worth", "dignity" and "rights" of the person. Third, humanism is "ethical", believing that morality is real as opposed to relative, "an intrinsic part of human nature based on understanding and a concern for others".

These are serious and important statements (which are unpacked in greater detail in the essay) and many Christians (and people of other religions) will agree with them. However, the contention of the second part of this essay is that this commitment to rationality, human dignity and moral realism is better founded on Christian beliefs and commitments than on atheistic ones.

It is important to be crystal clear at this point. To put forward this argument is not to claim that all Christians are necessarily humanists. Many, regrettably, are not. Nor is it to claim that only Christians can lay claim to the humanist label, let alone that non-Christian humanists are themselves in any way morally or rationally deficient. As the first chapter will make clear, humanism has the potential to be a broad ideological church in which people with different metaphysical commitments can share certain goals and ambitions for life and society. As Babu Goginieni, International Director of the International Humanist and Ethical Union recently remarked,

> the enemies of humanism are not only on the religious side… Atheism is not important. I happen to be an atheist, but that's not the point – what is important is freedom and human values, and a way of living with others and with nature.[3]

To raise questions about those different metaphysical commitments is not to undermine that capacity for collaboration. Rather, it is simply to make the narrower point that, ultimately, humanism, to be philosophically coherent and robust, needs theism.

This will, of course, be contested – and rightly so. To agree on shared humanistic objectives is not to impose consensus where there is none. But it may also be judged irrelevant. What does it matter, some will say, if some foundations for humanism are stronger than others? As long as people are building the same way, to the same ends, things should be fine.

There is an answer to this but unfortunately it often gets stuck with the Nazis or the Communists. It is, after all, within living memory that the best educated and most literate nation in Europe and their atheistic allies-turned-enemies in the east committed the most horrible crimes against humanity, utterly ignoring claims of human dignity in their pursuit of an alleged racial purity or social utopia. We should not ignore the warnings from history – or so this answer goes.

This is technically true but it is also unhelpfully hyperbolic. No one today is seriously claiming we face an imminent return to the horrors of recent history, let alone because our shared humanism is built on defective philosophical premises. Failing to recognise the surest foundations for human rationality, morality and dignity will not plunge us straight back into the anti-human nightmares of yesteryear.

However, just as the price of freedom is eternal vigilance, so the price of humanism is philosophical rigour. To fail to attend to the logical underpinning of humanism is to risk its imperceptibly slow decay, whether that is to the rot of overzealous 'postmodernism', suspicious of all truth claims; or to moral relativism, equally suspicious of moral truth claims; or to ethical systems in which commitment to, say, greatest happiness or personal freedom nibbles away at the edges of our unqualified commitment to human worth. Chapters two, three and four nod gently in the direction of where an inadequate attention to the philosophical foundations of humanism might, and in a few instances have, lead us – being careful to avoid scaremongering in the process.

# 2.

In 1928, T.S. Eliot wrote an essay on the humanism of the American literary critic Irving Babbitt. In it he observed that

> humanism is either an alternative to religion, or is ancillary to it. To my mind, it always flourishes most when religion has been strong; and if you find examples of humanism which are anti-religious, or at least in opposition to the religious faith of the place and time, then such humanism is purely destructive, for it has never found anything to replace what it destroyed.[4]

This clearly irked Babbit, who responded claiming that Eliot had "misstated" his views, thereby eliciting a reply from Eliot the following year.[5] In this Eliot claimed that his essay "was not intended to be an attack [on humanism]" but rather "to point out the weak points in its defences, before some genuine enemy took advantage of them." With some prescience he wrote that it was humanism's "positivistic tendencies" that were alarming, that it had a "tendency towards a positive and exclusive dogma". "Conceive a Comtism from which all the absurdities have been removed," he wrote (noting in parenthesis that "they form, I admit, a very important part of the Comtist scheme)", "and you have something like what I imagine Humanism might become". This was not, however, at least in Eliot's mind, a done deal. Humanism could still be inclusive. "There is no opposition between the religious and the pure humanistic attitude: they are necessary to each other."

This is also the point of this essay. We seek not to attack humanism but to affirm the deep affinities between it and Christianity, diverting it from any positivist or exclusive tendencies, while seeking to show how humanism needs Christianity in order to remain secure. It is written to point out – and to shore up – the weak points in its defences, before any genuine enemy takes advantage of them.

## introduction – references

1. Nicolas Walter, *Humanism: What's in the Word?* (London: Rationalist Press Association, 1997), p. 8. I am grateful to Andrew Copson of the British Humanist Association for bringing my attention to this unjustly neglected pamphlet.
2. Walter, *Humanism*, p. 10.
3. Quoted by Andrew Brown, 'Religion without a church? Humanism almost qualifies', *The Guardian*, Tuesday 12 August 2014: http://www.theguardian.com/commentisfree/2014/aug/12/religion-humanism-atheism
4. T.S. Eliot, *Selected Essays* (London: Faber and Faber, 1972), p. 475.
5. Eliot, *Selected Essays*, pp. 481-91.

# being generous with humanism

## 1.

We begin where we just ended, with T.S. Eliot. In his poem *Burnt Norton*, Eliot famously wrote that words "decay with imprecision, will not stay in place,/ Will not stay still."[1] So it is with 'humanism'. Historian Alan Bullock opened his book, *The Humanist Tradition in the West*, by attempting to define 'humanist' and 'humanism' before concluding that they are

> words that no one has ever succeeded in defining to anyone else's satisfaction, protean words which mean very different things to different people and leave lexicographers and encyclopaedists with a feeling of exasperation and frustration.[2]

The sentiment should serve as a salutary warning to anyone who thinks they have captured 'humanism', defining it clearly, precisely and unambiguously. The word, and the ideas behind it, has had a range of distinct meanings over the last 2,000 years and it is a brave – or hubristic – person who claims they have nailed the one true meaning. As Nicolas Walter remarks in his little book *Humanism: What's in the Word?*, published by the Rationalist Press Association, "attempts to control books and words almost never succeed."[3]

## 2.

Humanism's prehistory lies in the classical world, in the Latin term *humanitas* meaning human nature, in the sense of a civilized – as opposed to barbarian – human nature. Although sometimes used to mean philanthropy, it was more often deployed to indicate the kind of education that befitted a cultivated man. Because speech was what distinguished humans from animals, fine speech was an indication of superior humanity. *Humanitas* came to indicate the virtues of an educated and cultivated existence, especially as characterised and popularised by the much-admired orator and stylist Cicero.

It was this sense of 'humanism' that was adopted and developed in the Renaissance, although the word itself was yet to be coined. Rediscovery of classical texts in the libraries of ancient monasteries and the travel bags of Greek scholars fleeing the ruins of the

Byzantine empire effected a reconsideration of the Roman world. *Studia humanitatis*, the study of these texts primarily, at first, for their grammatical and rhetorical qualities, developed as a respected discipline, scholars of this bent being called 'umanista'.

Although there were tensions between this activity and more obviously theological scholasticism of the time – some humanists were among those who questioned the earthly use of such heavenly philosophy – the fact is that, in Diarmaid MacCulloch's words, "the vast majority of humanists were patently sincere Christians who wished to apply their enthusiasm to the exploration and proclamation of their faith."[4]

Renaissance humanism, it is also commonly claimed, also heralded, alongside its interest in classical grammar and rhetoric, a renewed focus on the dignity and potential of mankind. This appreciation is certainly palpable, most famously in Giovanni Pico della Mirandola's *On the Dignity of Man*, which is often quoted as the archetypal example of how the Renaissance re-evaluation of human nature, in the light of the classical world, elevated human nature to unprecedented heights.

The idea that this was a *new* conception is, however, more questionable and owes more to the later nineteenth century, when the Renaissance was first identified as a distinct historical movement, than it does to the movement itself. Although the Renaissance's sense of optimism about human nature and its social potential does stand in contrast to some of the rather more downbeat pronouncements of Reformed Protestantism, it is still of a piece with the longstanding idea of humans as divine image bearers. There is no straightforward or exclusive link between the 'humanism' of the Renaissance and the idea of human dignity.

The meaning of the word humanist – the word first appears in English in the later 16th century – subsequently oscillated between two similar definitions, namely someone who was essentially a practiced grammarian or rhetorician and someone who was a student of human affairs. In the first category, Samuel Johnson defined a humanist in his *Dictionary* of 1755 as "a philologer, a grammarian".[5] In the second, the Elizabethan traveller and writer Fynes Moryson, defined one as "him that affects the knowledge of State affaires, Histories, Cosmography, and the like."[6] When the first publication to be titled *The Humanist* was published in 1757, the editor, an Irish clergyman, wrote that "the title…implies neither more nor less, than that it interests itself in all the concerns of human nature", and claimed that the magazine was "calculated to convey some little useful and entertaining knowledge of various kinds, historical, classical, natural, moral, and *now-and-then* a *little religion* into the readers' minds". Sadly it lasted only 15 issues. It is these two meanings that still dominate in the Oxford English Dictionary, covering three of its five definitions of the word. In its origins, there was certainly no sense that humanism or humanists were being anti-religious, even among the various small groups of anti-clerical freethinkers, sceptics and atheists of the later eighteenth century.

## 3.

The original, educational sense of the word gained strength in the early nineteenth century, when the Bavarian educational commissioner Friedrich Niethammer coined the word *humanismus* to describe the classical education he planned for German schools, a pedagogy whose basic characteristic was always "to care more for the humanity than for the Animality of the pupil".[7]

The idea of 'humanism' retained this pedagogical emphasis throughout the century, but the word itself refused to stay still, and took on a more complex set of connotations when it was picked up by historians, such as Georg Voigt and Jacob Burckhardt, to describe the ideology of the Italian Renaissance.

It was here the idea that the Renaissance constituted a complete break with the (so called) middle ages was established as a truism. It was here the idea, in historian J.A. Symonds' words of 1877, that "the essence of humanism consisted in a new and vital perception of the dignity of man as a rational being apart from theological considerations" was born.[8] And it was here that the tensions between scholastic and humanist scholarship were "reinterpreted as doctrinal controversy between theistic and humanistic belief".[9] This newly modified idea of humanism was, in Nicolas Walters' words, "applied retrospectively and indeed anachronistically and unhistorically".[10]

It was in this context of the expansion and manipulation of the idea of humanism in the later 19th century that a more anti-religious sense developed. This sense existed, at least latently, from earlier in the century. As early as 1812, the word 'humanism' could be used in the sense of 'not Christian', as when Samuel Taylor Coleridge wrote of the one "who has passed from orthodoxy to the loosest Arminianism, and thence to Arianism, and thence to direct humanism [before falling] off into the hopeless abyss of atheism." The humanist, in this sense, was not anti-religious but, in effect, a deist or Unitarian, a believer in God but without any doctrinal trappings.[11]

It was the disciples of the philosopher Georg Hegel, known as the Young or Left Hegelians, who first introduced a more specific non-Christian element to the idea of humanism, in the second quarter of the 19th century. One of the more prominent, Ludwig Feuerbach, explicitly put humanity in God's position, as the object worthy of reverence, but it was his contemporary, Arnold Ruge, who adopted humanism, alongside other terms like Anthropotheism, to describe this shift.

Ruge adopted this basic idea and built from it the idea of humanism as a religion. "As soon as this meaning of Christianism is discovered, the whole Christian heaven falls to the earth, and a new religion is originated, the religion of Humanism", he wrote.[12] Modelled as this humanism was on the Christian template, it had an eschatological, even utopian, tinge to it. Humanism was, in effect, the culmination of Christianity. "The old form of religion is Christian belief, or old Christianity; the new religion is realised Christianity, or Humanism", he wrote, in a sentence that was suppressed when the essay in which it appears was originally published in 1841.[13]

Feuerbach and Ruge conceived humanism as a religious alternative to Christianity. Others were more stridently anti-Christian, denouncing any religious associations. Karl Marx and Friedrich Engels bitterly criticised the idea that humanism might involve any religious elements at all and the early anarchist Pierre-Joseph Proudhon complained that "humanism is a religion as detestable as any of the theisms of ancient origin", and even said that it was necessary to "reject humanism" because it "tended invincibly, by the deification of humanity, to a religious restoration".[14] The Russian revolutionary Michael Bakunin, wrote, in 1843, about how "a great enthusiasm for Humanism and for the State… [and] a burning hatred of priests and their impudent defilement of all that is humanly great and true, again fills the world."[15]

Such fiercely anti-Christian humanist sentiments were the exception rather than the rule, however. Ruge was more typical when he wrote in 1850 that "real humanism has to abolish neither philosophy nor religion", and issued a clarion call which sounded that note: "Let the philosophical humanism join the religious humanism! The one great cause… the realisation of humanity and Christianity".[16]

## 4.

Ruge's talk of "a human religion" and "the invisible church of humanity" informed a brief humanistic religious association in Europe but neither it, nor he, had much impact – certainly not as much as the contemporary French thinkers, like Henri de Saint-Simon and Auguste Comte, who developed a full-blooded religion of humanity that was to be longer lasting.

This movement sought to deify humanity more explicitly and more colourfully than anything Ruge attempted, causing mirth among many critics, not least the biologist T.H. Huxley who witheringly, if accurately, described it as "Catholicism minus Christianity". The movement was usually termed Positivism but was sometimes called humanism, such as by William Gladstone, who referred to "Positivism or Comtism, or, as it might be called, Humanism"[17] or the linguist and scholar, Ernest Renan, who wrote in 1848, "it is my deep conviction that pure *humanism* will be the religion of the future, that is, the cult of all that pertains to man."[18]

It was possibly because of these religious associations that the great anti-Christian figures of 19th century Britain, such as George Holyoake, Charles Bradlaugh, George Foote and Chapman Cohen, rarely used the word humanism to describe their beliefs or activities, preferring instead to talk of free-thought, atheism, naturalism, rationalism, or secularism. As Nicolas Walter remarks, "the freethought movement was in general indifferent or opposed to Humanism well into the 20th century".[19]

Positivism, in its early, French, incarnation, had limited impact in Britain. Richard Congreve, a history fellow at Wadham College, Oxford, joined the movement in 1854, and was nominated by Comte as the "spontaneous leader" of British positivists. He converted several of his students and they went on to found the London Positivist Society in 1867, with the ambition to replace the Church of England with the religion of humanity, as Comte had envisaged he would do with the Roman Catholic Church in France. Although the movement influenced some key figures, such as John Stuart Mill and George Eliot, it soon split, with one splinter going on to become the kernel of what would be called the 'Ethical Movement'.

This retained many of the religious overtones and ideas of its parent movement. When *The Humanist*, the organ of the ethical movement, was published in the 1920s, the front page editorial of the first issue was on "The Religion of Humanism" which was based on "faith in man". "Faith is indispensible, for Humanism as for every other religion" opined legal scholar Robert K. Wilson in 1919.[20]

Even those self-proclaimed rationalists, more naturally antagonistic to the religious origins and feel of the ethical movement, spoke of humanism in religious terms. "Humanism!" exclaimed Charles Hooper, first secretary of the Rationalist Press Association in 1900, "What one word could be better adapted to mark the gospel which is a gospel at once of human knowledge, of human nature, and of human society?."[21]

This did not, of course, mean that humanism was necessarily theistic. Indeed, some, like F.J. Gould, a co-founder of the Rationalist Press Association, in 1900 saw in humanism "a new idea [that] is actually displacing Theism… [that] lies in the contrast with Theism".[22] Nor should the repeated religious rhetoric be taken to indicate that humanism was in deemed to be unscientific. A number of thinkers, most prominently Julian Huxley, explicitly married science and humanism in the idea of scientific – or 'evolutionary' or 'trans' – humanism, emphasising that humanism meant "human control by human effort in accordance with human ideas" with the objective that ultimately "the human species can, if it wishes, transcend itself… in its entirety, as humanity."[23]

> *Right the way up the middle of the 20th century (and beyond) humanism was understood to encompass a range of positions, a generous and inclusive family of ideas, rather than a single, narrow movement.*

Rather it is an indication that right the way up the middle of the 20th century (and beyond) humanism was understood to encompass a range of positions, a generous and inclusive family of ideas, rather than a single, narrow movement. In the words of S.H. Swinny, then President of the London Positivist Society and editor of the Positivist Review, "we certainly claim no proprietary right in the word Humanist [and] we welcome all to the Humanist name."[24]

When, in 1944, the BBC put on three talks about humanism it engaged with scientific humanism (with Julian Huxley), classical humanism (with Gilbert Murray) and Christian Humanism (with J.H. Oldham). The three did not agree on everything – Oldham, for example, insisted that humanism needed theism whilst Huxley argued "that humanism was the basis for a definite organised religion" – but there was little sense that, awkward bedfellows though they might sometime be, divorce was imminent.

## 5.

The fact that it was, was due in some measure to Christians rather than atheists. In 1945, the Church of England report *Towards the Conversion of England*, took several side-swipes at 'humanism' choosing to understand it in its narrow and more intolerant form. "Humanism is the word now commonly used to describe that view of life which sees in man the source of all meaning and value, instead of God", the report wrote, with only partial truth.[25] Such an interpretation helped effect a detachment and then separation, which was further ensured by the educationalist Harold Blackham, who helped steer the ethical movement away from its religious forms, and the psychologist Margaret Knight, whose 1955 BBC broadcasts on 'Morals without Religion' created a storm of protest.

"Humanism", Blackham bluntly stated in 1967, "[is] an alternative to religion".[26] It proceeds "from the assumptions that man is on his own and this life is all and as assumption of responsibility for one's life and for the life of mankind".[27]

> It is a decision, a commitment, a faith… the slow growth of secular self-confidence…[a] turn to even more dazzling prospects in the open future: it is this secularism, this religion of progress, which has come to be called humanism.[28]

At the same time, the generous and inclusive understanding of humanism that had characterised the pre-war world was fading. On the one hand, the tradition of classical humanism, so long the foundation stone of humanism, crumbled away as classicism fell out of favour in post-war educational circles. On the other, the tradition of Christian humanism also fell strangely silent. Whereas the interwar years had seen publications like the *Humanism and the Bible* series, with titles like *Evangelical Humanism* and *Studies in Old Testament Humanism* coming from Protestant circles, and the work of the French neo-Thomist philosopher Jacques Maritain, who published his book *True* (later *Integral*) *Humanism* in 1938, being read in Catholic circles, post-war Christian thinkers seemed more ambivalent about the label, allowing it to become narrower and more exclusive than it had heretofore been.

It may be that this is only a temporary drift in the word's meanings. Nicolas Walter writes of religious humanism, scientific humanism, secular humanism, ethical humanism, and rationalist humanism. Other scholars speak of romantic humanism, existential humanism, dialogic humanism, civic humanism, spiritual humanism, pagan humanism, pragmatic humanism, and technological humanism.[29] However, such subtleties are restricted to seminar rooms. Among the wider public it seems that the idea, expressed by Stanton Coit, leading light of the ethical movement, that "within humanism there are many points of view", is incomprehensible.[30]

# 6.

It is hoped that this brief account of the history of humanism has shown that idea, that "within humanism there are many points of view", is not, in fact, incomprehensible. For most of its history, 'humanism' has been a broad church, and Christianity and humanism have been anything but enemies. Not only is it quite possible to 'do both', but the very idea that there was some kind of irreconcilable antagonism between the two is a very recent invention, which would have been anathema to most humanists through history. As Nicolas Walter has noted,

> *For most of its history, 'humanism' has been a broad church, and Christianity and humanism have been anything but enemies.*

> it is only half a century since we [meaning rationalists/atheists] took over words which for several centuries had already been used by other kinds of people with other kinds of meanings, so that we may just as well be accused of stealing them as anyone else.[31]

That recognised, it is those who have appropriated the term most enthusiastically over recent decades, to whom most attention should be paid. Just because humanism has been a broad and inclusive term in the past, or has meant a whole range of things including "devotion to human interests" or "those studies which promote human culture", that does not mean it still does.[32] One should avoid the etymological fallacy – the idea that a word necessarily means today what is meant in the past – and seek to understand words and ideas as they are currently deployed.

Two caveats are worth noting at this point. The first pertains to Nicolas Walter's remark, quoted earlier, that attempts to control books and words almost never succeed. Whilst it is entirely right to seek to understand words and ideas as they are actually used, the fact is that different people use them in different ways for perfectly good reasons, and to circumscribe or de-legitimise alternative usages in favour of the one holy catholic and apostolic meaning is problematic. Such was the story of miaphysite Christianity with which this essay began. As Walter rightly remarks,

> many if not most of the people who have called themselves or have been called Humanists at any time would reject some if not most of the dozen propositions contained in either version of the [official] Minimum statement.[33]

That, however, does not delegitimise their use of that term.

The second caveat, closely linked to the first, is that many of the more formal or official pronouncements about humanism over recent years have recognised that the term is elastic and protean, and does not demand strict and unwavering adherence to a certain number of propositions. For example, Richard Norman, a founder-member of the Humanist Philosophers' Group, and a Vice-President of the British Humanist Association, wrote in his book *On Humanism*, "there is no humanist creed, no set of beliefs to which every humanist has to subscribe".[34] Rather, he continues, "I do not think there is any definitive set of beliefs called 'humanism'. There are many humanisms."[35] Similarly, the important Amsterdam Declaration of the International Humanist and Ethical Union (IHEU), to which we shall return presently, declares in the fourth of its seven "fundamental" propositions, "humanism is undogmatic, imposing no creed upon its adherents."[36]

Bearing these caveats in mind, we will look at the modern, "exclusive" definitions of humanism in an attempt to understand what it entails.[37] A number of themes run through the definitions and characterizations of humanism that are offered by prominent, self-proclaimed humanists. One is that humanism entails being good without the need for divine carrots or sticks. Thus, the novelist Kurt Vonnegut wrote that "being a humanist means trying to behave decently without expectation of rewards or punishment after you are dead," and Jim Al-Khalili, President of the British Humanist Association, said that reason, decency, tolerance, empathy and hope are human traits that we should aspire to, not because we seek reward of eternal life or because we fear the punishment of a supernatural being, but because they define our humanity.

A second theme is one of "the intense wonder and beauty of the universe", in the words of Professor Brian Cox, or "a strong sense of awe and wonder in the world" (Al-Khalili again). Having a powerful sense of the beauty and wonders of the natural world and universe is clearly an important part of being a humanist.

A third is the emphasis on human agency and potential. "I'm responsible, there is a meaning, and it is to make things better and to work for greater good and greater wisdom," wrote the noted humanist author, Philip Pullman. Or, in the words of humanist paterfamilias Harold Blackhan,

> life is not presented by Humanism as something for our judgement, something finished, take it or leave it. It is presented as raw material for our creative use, a task for our responsible undertaking.

A fourth theme is that of the importance of free intellectual enquiry. "All children should be free to grow up in a world where they are allowed to question, doubt, think freely and reach their own conclusions about what they believe", wrote humanist and comedian Ariane Sherine. Humanists clearly place stress on genuine intellectual inquiry.[38]

If these are the central definitions and characterisations of humanism, however, they would include pretty much every orthodox Christian theist on the planet. The idea that Christian ethics is based on divine reward or punishment is a caricature that does not bear much scrutiny, as any textbook on Christian ethics will show. Christians believe they should be good because humans are intrinsically moral creatures, because they operate within an objective moral order, because they are loved, and because they are forgiven – not because they are threatened or rewarded for being so.[39]

The idea that believing in God somehow immunises you to "the intense wonder and beauty of the universe" is an obvious untruth, as even a cursory glance at, for example, the books of Psalms shows. Theism does not blind you to the wonders of creation.

The idea that humans are 'responsible' beings, mandated to work for the common good is foundational to the Christian narrative, from the commission in Eden to the Sermon on the Mount. Indeed, it was liberation from the unalterable fate that was supposedly written in the stars that was one of Christianity's most abrasive challenges to the ancient world. It is true that mainstream Christian thought might cavil at some of the more hubristic claims of human potential – we are mandated to work for greater good but may be disappointed with how much we actually achieve – but the fundamental point that humans have a commission to be responsible for the good of creation remains central to Christian thought.

Lastly, the idea that Christian children (or indeed adults) should be prevented from genuine intellectual enquiry is essentially a parody, which pays scant attention to the monastic preservation of the classical world in the first millennium, the church's subsequent foundation of Europe's leading universities, the intellectual foundations of the scientific revolution in the 17th century, the church's role in founding national schooling in Britain, and the positive attitude to wisdom that pervades Christian scripture, tradition and practice.

Overall, therefore, while it is presumably possible to find examples of Christians who have contravened all these points – who believe that the goodness demands God standing over you with a big stick; who are indifferent to the wonders, and the good, of creation; and who eschew genuine intellectual enquiry – they are hardly reflective of orthodox Christian thought and practice. On the basis of these descriptions, therefore, humanism is wholly consonant with Christianity.

That recognised, to take these descriptions alone might lay us open to the accusation of cherry-picking those definitions and characterisations that were most obviously consonant and therefore best suited our argument. Moreover, it would be entirely fair to point out that none of the descriptions offered above is exactly systematic or detailed. Is there no more 'official' definition of humanism we might use?

# 7.

In response to this, we can turn to the 2002 Amsterdam Declaration of the International Humanist and Ethical Union, "the fullest definition to have a measure of international agreement" according to the BHA. This was developed on the 50th anniversary of the first World Humanist Congress and the original Amsterdam Declaration, and was "adopted unanimously" by the IHEU General Assembly, "and thus became the official defining statement of World Humanism". This fascinating and important text is worth quoting in full:

> The fundamentals of modern Humanism are as follows:
> 
> 1. Humanism is ethical. It affirms the worth, dignity and autonomy of the individual and the right of every human being to the greatest possible freedom compatible with the rights of others. Humanists have a duty of

care to all of humanity including future generations. Humanists believe that morality is an intrinsic part of human nature based on understanding and a concern for others, needing no external sanction.

2. Humanism is rational. It seeks to use science creatively, not destructively. Humanists believe that the solutions to the world's problems lie in human thought and action rather than divine intervention. Humanism advocates the application of the methods of science and free inquiry to the problems of human welfare. But Humanists also believe that the application of science and technology must be tempered by human values. Science gives us the means but human values must propose the ends.

3. Humanism supports democracy and human rights. Humanism aims at the fullest possible development of every human being. It holds that democracy and human development are matters of right. The principles of democracy and human rights can be applied to many human relationships and are not restricted to methods of government.

4. Humanism insists that personal liberty must be combined with social responsibility. Humanism ventures to build a world on the idea of the free person responsible to society, and recognises our dependence on and responsibility for the natural world. Humanism is undogmatic, imposing no creed upon its adherents. It is thus committed to education free from indoctrination.

5. Humanism is a response to the widespread demand for an alternative to dogmatic religion. The world's major religions claim to be based on revelations fixed for all time, and many seek to impose their world-views on all of humanity. Humanism recognises that reliable knowledge of the world and ourselves arises through a continuing process of observation, evaluation and revision.

6. Humanism values artistic creativity and imagination and recognises the transforming power of art. Humanism affirms the importance of literature, music, and the visual and performing arts for personal development and fulfilment.

7. Humanism is a lifestance aiming at the maximum possible fulfilment through the cultivation of ethical and creative living and offers an ethical and rational means of addressing the challenges of our times. Humanism can be a way of life for everyone everywhere.

> Our primary task is to make human beings aware in the simplest terms of what Humanism can mean to them and what it commits them to. By utilising free inquiry, the power of science and creative imagination for the furtherance of peace and in the service of compassion, we have confidence that we have the means to solve the problems that confront us all. We call upon all who share this conviction to associate themselves with us in this endeavour. [40]

There is a great deal that might be said about this fascinating set of 'fundamentals' (perhaps an odd word to choose given its connotations with 'fundamentalism'), but for the sake of brevity we would like to point out five at this juncture.

The first, which has already been noted, is that "humanism is undogmatic, imposing no creed upon its adherents". This may seem like an odd statement to make half way through a list of 'fundamentals' but it is a crucial one nonetheless, and concurs with other observations about the breadth of the term 'humanism'. It is one to which we shall return.

Second, this list of fundamentals is refreshingly free of caricature and parody and seeks not to define humanism over and against religion, let alone a cartoon version of religion. The single article that does deal with religion is fair-minded and accurate: it is, after all, certainly true that many (or at least some) religions (or at least religious groups) "seek to impose their world-views", and true that humanism has an appeal to many as "an alternative to dogmatic religion."

Third, there are certainly propositions within this declaration that would be problematic for Christian believers, or at least for Christian theists. Most obvious among these is the statement that "the solutions to the world's problems lie in human thought and action rather than divine intervention." That noted, even those Christian theists who are more prominent in their expectation of "divine intervention" would not deny that the solutions to the world's problems also lie in human thought and action. For them it would be both/and, rather than either/or.

Such dissimilarities noted, there are fewer than one might expect, which leads on to a fourth point, namely that the declaration eschews explicitly anti-religious rhetoric or claims. It does not say, as one might expect, that humanism is an anti- or non-religious creed. It does not say, like the 1991 IHEU Minimum Statement that humanism "is not theistic". Nor, even, does it seek to make metaphysical points about naturalism as the basis for all thought. Some definitions do do this. Both the Oxford Companion to Philosophy and the Cambridge Dictionary of Philosophy contain (elements of) a definition that are in contrast to (elements of) religion: humanism is an appeal to reason *in contrast to revelation or religious authority* as a means of finding out about the natural world and destiny of man... Believing that it is possible to live confidently *without metaphysical or religious certainty*...[41]

Such definitions are clearly more problematic for mainstream Christian theists, but it is noteworthy that the IHEU Amsterdam statement avoids them altogether.

This is not as noteworthy, however, as the fifth point which is quite how much in the Amsterdam definition mainstream Christian theists would wholeheartedly countersign. Thus, appropriating the language of the declaration we can confidently say that:

- Christianity affirms the worth and dignity of the individual and the right of every human being to the greatest possible freedom compatible with the rights of others.

- Christians believe they have a duty of care to all of humanity including future generations.

- Christians believe that morality is an intrinsic part of human nature.

- Christianity seeks to use science creatively, not destructively, and advocates the application of the methods of science and free inquiry to the problems of human welfare, in such a way as is tempered by human values.

- Christianity supports democracy and human rights, and aims at the fullest possible development of every human being. It holds that democracy and human development are matters of right, and are not restricted to methods of government.

- Christianity insists that personal liberty must be combined with social responsibility, recognising our dependence on and responsibility for the natural world.

- Christianity recognises that reliable knowledge of the world and ourselves arises through a continuing process of observation, evaluation and revision.

- Christianity values artistic creativity and imagination and recognises the transforming power of art. It affirms the importance of literature, music, and the visual and performing arts for personal development and fulfilment.

- Christianity is a lifestance, a way of life for everyone everywhere, aiming at the maximum possible fulfilment through the cultivation of ethical and creative living and offers an ethical and rational means of addressing the challenges of our times.

This litany could be extended but the point should be clear. Whilst there are elements of the humanism outlined in the Amsterdam Declaration that mainstream Christians might find uncomfortable or would be inclined to rephrase, the broad consensus between Christianity and humanism is obvious.

## 8.

To return, then, to the main point of this chapter: were it the case that humanism had a strict and particular set of creeds, all of which an individual needed to countersign in order to claim the name humanist, mainstream Christian theists would have some difficulty in calling themselves humanists, at least in the modern sense of the word. If, for example, the statement, "humanism is not theistic" was front and centre of the Amsterdam Declaration, that would make it impossible for all but the most fringe Christians to sign up to it.

However, quite apart from the fact that until recently humanism was a generous and broad church that was perfectly happy to accommodate people of religious faith and none, contemporary, authoritative descriptions of humanism are repeatedly at pains to emphasise that this is not the case and that humanism, properly understood is about reason, ethics, dignity, liberty, equality, responsibility, etc., rather than simply the rejection of God. The sheer range of the similarities between the fundamentals outlined in IHEU Amsterdam Declaration and mainstream Christian commitments powerfully suggests that even in its modern, more exclusive incarnation – as opposed to the more generous, historical one – it is entirely right for Christians to be humanists.

## 9.

This, then, is the first part of the claim of this volume, namely that Christians can be humanists.

It is only the first part, however, and leads on to a second, more contentious claim. This is not simply that Christians can be humanists but that they *must* be humanists because an atheistic conception of reality is insufficiently robust to sustain commitments such as those laid out in the Amsterdam declaration.

Which commitments? The discussion above should give some indication of quite how much overlap there is between Christianity and humanism and it should, accordingly, be possible to select quite a number of potential categories to analyse. However, we have elected to look at three 'fundamentals' that seem (to us) to be of foundational importance. These are (in the order we shall analyse them, rather than the order they appear in the Amsterdam declaration):

Firstly, humanism is "rational" (Point 2). It recognises that "reliable knowledge of the world and ourselves arises through a continuing process of observation, evaluation and revision" (Point 5). It believes that "the solutions to the world's problems lie in human thought and action" (2) by "the application of the methods of science and free inquiry to the problems of human welfare", albeit "tempered by human values" (2).

Second, humanism affirms human dignity. It is committed to the "worth", "dignity" and "rights" of the person (Point 1). It supports the idea of human rights and aims "at the fullest possible development of every human being", holding that "the principles of… human rights can be applied to many human relationships and are not restricted to methods of government" (Point 3).

> *Atheism saws through the branch on which humanism sits.*

Third, humanism is "ethical" (Point 1). It believes that morality is real, as opposed to relative or fabricated ("morality is an intrinsic part of human nature based on understanding and a concern for others") and that humanists have moral duties not just to themselves or their families but "a duty of care to all of humanity including future generations".

It is our contention that this commitment to rationality, morality and human dignity is not simply wholly good and merits the unqualified support of Christians but that only belief in God can provide a sufficiently robust philosophical foundation to sustain these claims. This is not, it should be made crystal clear, to claim that only Christian humanists are moral, rational or have a commitment to human dignity; or that all Christian humanists are moral, rational or have a commitment to human dignity; or that no atheist humanists are moral, rational or have a commitment to human dignity. Nothing that follows constitutes a theoretical or empirical claim pertaining to any of these points.

Rather, the argument is simply that many of the 'fundamentals' of humanism find their origins in Christian thought and commitments and that these fundamentals can ultimately only be sustained by those faith commitments; or, more directly, atheism saws through the branch on which humanism sits.

This is obviously a more contentious claim than has been made in this opening chapter, and so the remaining chapters of this essay will set out to outline and justify it, beginning first with rationality, before moving on to dignity and morality.

## chapter 1 – references

1. T.S. Eliot, Complete Poems (London: Faber and Faber, 1963), p. 194.
2. Alan Bullock, *The Humanist Tradition in the West* (New York; London : Norton, 1985), p. 8.
3. Walter, *Humanism*, p. 8.
4. Diarmaid MacCulloch, *A History of Christianity: The First Three Thousand Years* (London: Penguin, 2010) p. 574.
5. Oxford English Dictionary, (Oxford, 1989; 2nd ed.), Vol. VIII, p. 475.
6. Oxford English Dictionary, op. cit., p. 475; Walter, p. 14.
7. Quoted in Walter, p. 18.
8. J.A. Symonds, *Renaissance in Italy, Book II, The Revival of Learning*, (London: Smith, Elder & Co., 1875-86).
9. Walter, p. 21.
10. Walter, p. 21.
11. Joseph Cottle, *Early Recollections: Chiefly Relating to the Late Samuel Taylor* (London: Longman, Rees & Co. and Hamilton Adams & Co, 1837), Volume 2, p. 121.
12. Walter, p. 26.
13. Walter, p. 24.
14. Walter, p. 29.
15. Walter, p. 25.
16. Walter, p. 26.
17. Walter, p. 31.
18. Quoted in Vito R. Giustiniani, 'Homo, Humanus, and the Meanings of Humanism', in *Journal of the History of Ideas*, Vol. 46, No. 2 (Apr. - Jun., 1985), pp. 167-195.
19. Walter, p. 42.
20. Walter, p. 46.
21. Walter, p. 44.
22. Walter, p. 46.
23. Julian Huxley, *New Bottles for New Wine* (London: Chatto & Windus, 1957).
24. Walter, p. 47.
25. Walter, p. 61.
26. Harold Blackham, *Monthly Record*, January 1967.
27. Harold Blackham, *Humanism* (Harmondsworth: Penguin Books, 1968), p. 13.
28. Walter, p. 63.
29. See Martin Halliwell and Andy Mousley, *Critical Humanisms: Humanist/Anti-humanist Dialogues* (Edinburgh University Press, 2003).

30  Walter, p. 45.
31  Walter, p. 10.
32  As it happens both of these phrases are current and have definitions according to the Oxford English Dictionary, but the point still stands.
33  Walter, p.9. The Minimum Statement was drafted, adopted and issued by the IHEU in 1991 and subsequently amended, by the insertion of a sentence [here in brackets] by the IHEU Board five years later. It reads:

> Humanism is a democratic and ethical life stance, which affirms that human beings have the right and responsibility to give meaning and shape to their own lives. [It stands for the building of a more humane society through an ethic based on human and other natural values in the spirit of reason and free inquiry through human capabilities.] It is not theistic, and it does not accept supernatural views of reality.

The final sentence would obviously bar all mainstream Christians from claiming the name humanist, but as we shall see, this explicit association of humanism with atheism is rare in humanist creeds.

34  Richard Norman, *On Humanism* (Abingdon, Oxford; New York: Routledge, 2012), p. 24.
35  Norman, *On Humanism*, p. 8.
36  There are some indications that this is not so and that organised humanism may not be quite as fluid and inclusive as all that. The IHEU has a detailed page outlining its bylaws, which it separates into a "three-layer Bylaws structure", namely "the basic regulations on what the IHEU is…Internal Rules…[and] Specific Rules." Some details are available here – http://iheu.org/iheu-bylaws/ – although at the time of writing the pages detailing the different levels of bylaws were unavailable and it was not, therefore, clear whether "All member organisations of the International Humanist and Ethical Union are required by IHEU bylaw 5.1 to accept the IHEU Minimum Statement on Humanism", as Wikipedia claims.
37  "Exclusive humanism" is the term that Charles Taylor deploys in *A Secular Age* (Cambridge, Mass.; London: Belknap, 2007).
38  All quotes taken from the website of the British Humanist Association (see www.humanism.org.uk).
39  It is a common misconception among non-Christians, no doubt fed by the occasional bad sermon, that heaven is a reward for being good. It isn't.
40  'The Amsterdam Declaration 2002' Inernational Humanist Ethical Union. Available online at: http://iheu.org/humanism/the-amsterdam-declaration/
41  Emphases added. It is worth noting that these definitions are in contrast to the Concise Routledge Encyclopedia of Philosophy, also quoted by the BHA, which does not define humanism explicitly against religion: "…a commitment to the perspective, interests and centrality of human persons; a belief in reason and autonomy as foundational aspects of human existence; a belief that reason, scepticism and the scientific method are the only appropriate instruments for discovering truth and structuring the human community; a belief that the foundations for ethics and society are to be found in autonomy and moral equality…"

# 2

# why reason?

## 1.

Humanists view reason as a reliable way of getting to the truth. Atheist humanists often take this to be a point of contrast with religious believers (hence some of the hostility some of them show to the idea of a *Christian* humanism). On the British Humanist Association website, Stephen Law has written that

> Theists use the term "faith" as a tool by which they can, quite unfairly, avoid justifying their belief and sidestep awkward atheistic arguments ("But belief in God is a matter of faith, not reason!"), to disguise the fact that atheism is *far, far* more reasonable than theism.[1]

Richard Dawkins is characteristically strident on the subject:

> If children understand that beliefs should be substantiated with evidence, as opposed to tradition, authority, revelation or faith, they will automatically work out for themselves that they are atheists.[2]

These two quotations typify a cast of mind: that Christian faith is incompatible with a positive view of reason, and must instead rely only on "tradition, authority, revelation or faith."

This chapter will challenge that assumption. It will seek to show that Christians have a long tradition – stretching back to the very first century of the church's life – of valuing reason as a gift given by God to all people, whether or not they are believers. In fact, it will argue, atheist humanism has more difficulty accounting for its trust in reason. This is because it lacks a credible explanation of why human beings are able to reason in ways that track the truth.

Christian humanists believe that the universe is the creation of a benevolent God. If they are correct, this fact helps explain why the human mind should be able to reason (however fallibly) in ways that lead towards the truth. On the Christian account, human beings are right to trust what our faculties of reasoning do because they have been made to track the truth.

It is more difficult for atheist humanists to explain why human reason is trustworthy, for atheists have a very different understanding of the ultimate cause of human beings – and therefore a subtly different understanding of human nature. On their account, the human faculties of reasoning have evolved in an otherwise purposeless universe. The process of evolution selects for properties that are useful to a species. More specifically, it selects for properties that help that species to survive and replicate. Therefore, on an atheist account, we humans should expect our faculties of reason to be *useful*. But, of course, that is not the same thing as being *reliable*. Our faculties of reason may help us to survive and replicate – but why should we trust them as a vehicle for getting to the truth?

> On an atheist account, we humans should expect our faculties of reason to be useful. But, of course, that is not the same thing as being reliable.

This is the question posed by the Oxford philosopher Ralph Walker.[3] Walker's claim is that atheist humanism may cut off the very branch it needs to sit on; that is to say, its account of how our powers of reasoning emerged undermines our grounds for trusting those powers.

The *Guardian's* Andrew Brown summarises Walker's argument, and its implications:

> One of the oddest things about evolution is the fact we know that it's true. Odder still is the fact that we think it's important. This knowledge is almost entirely useless for our survival, or at least it has been up until very recently, yet we care about it passionately.
>
> Why on earth (where evolution rules) should abstract truth be so important to us? Why should it be even comprehensible? Why on earth would it be to the advantage of a creature to care about the truth in abstract, or to have a grasp of logic, or mathematics? All these capacities had clearly evolved in us long before they were useful.[4]

Of course, Brown observes, there are some who don't think reason is directed towards truth. On this view, our so-called knowledge is just a set of "helpful cognitive tricks that we have stumbled on" – helpful in the sense that they enable us to survive and replicate, and not that they reflect any kind of objective reality.

The problem with that view, however, is that it undermines itself. The very reasons that we use to get to the conclusion that reason is a set of "helpful cognitive tricks" would count for nothing if reason wasn't directed to the truth. If we are going to reason or argue at all from the scientific evidence, we have to trust that our faculties of reasoning in these complex and abstract areas are themselves reliable.

Christian and atheist humanists both reject the idea that reason is just a set of "helpful cognitive tricks." Both groups think reason is (to some extent) a trustworthy guide to the nature of reality. As we saw in the last chapter, the 2002 Amsterdam Declaration of the International Humanist and Ethical Union says that humanism is "rational". It recognises that *"reliable* knowledge of the world and ourselves arises through a continuing process of observation, evaluation and revision" (emphasis added).

Christian humanists are also in the happy position of being able to agree that reason can give us "reliable knowledge of the world and ourselves". Indeed, Christians go even further: from the earliest days of the Christian faith, Christians have been happy to give an explanation of why our capacities for reasoning provide such "reliable knowledge of the world".

In this chapter, we will discuss the story Christianity tells about reason and its reliability. We will show that there is a tradition of Christian thought, part of the tradition of Christian humanism we are discussing in this essay, which holds reason in high esteem, but which (in contrast to the kind of atheistic humanism advocated by Dawkins, above) is also aware of human frailty, and of our capacity for self-delusion. We will then consider the position of atheist humanism, and will show why Ralph Walker's arguments pose a serious challenge to that position. We will explain why we believe atheist humanism does indeed cut off the branch it is sitting on. The principles of reason themselves demand that we do not simply posit vast cosmic coincidences, and yet (we will argue) atheist humanists must see the reliability of human reason as a massive piece of good fortune.

## 2.

Justin Martyr lived from around 100 to 160 AD. His three surviving works (the first and second *Apologies* and the *Dialogue with Tryphon*) argue that Christianity is the true fulfilment of all philosophy, because the human capacity for reasoning is in fact a reflection of the divine reason (*logos*) which has become flesh in Jesus Christ.

For Christians, it is because human beings bear "the image and likeness" of God that our powers of reasoning are reliable – and, indeed, the limitations on that reliability come about because that image has been damaged.

Different Christians have different understandings of precisely how and to what extent our capacity for reasoning has been damaged. However, their recognition that our human reasoning is distorted by sin (that is, our state of separation from God) has an echo in the ways in which secular theorists acknowledge that both our material self-interest and our psychological needs and impulses distort our reasoning.[5] While they tell very different metaphysical stories, Christians and atheists alike have ample access to the empirical evidence of the impact of self-interest and self-deception on our capacity to reason and judge well. For Christian and atheist alike, it is therefore reasonable to have some humility about our capacity to reason.

As Justin Martyr emphasises, Christians have a positive (though not uncritical) estimation the rational capacities of the whole human race, not just those who believe.[6] To believe that human beings are made in the "image and likeness of God" is to believe that our finite nature shares something of the beauty, goodness and truth of the infinite God. For Justin Martyr, our reason (*logos*) shares – however imperfectly – in the *Logos* at the very heart of God.

It was this logic that underpinned the early scientific thinking of the seventeenth century. It was precisely because human reason was thought to in some way echo and participate in the reason of God – and because the world around us was taken to be rationally ordered – that humans had the confidence that the world should be comprehensible and explicable.[7]

Contemporary Catholic thought both draws on and develops this positive account of human reason.[8] In his encyclical on *Faith and Reason*, Pope John Paul II cites Justin Martyr as "a pioneer of positive engagement with philosophical thinking – albeit with cautious discernment." After surveying the history of Catholic teaching on the subject (most notably, that of Thomas Aquinas), John Paul II offers teaching for today's Catholics on how they should regard philosophy. He writes that:

> even when it engages theology, philosophy must remain faithful to its own principles and methods. Otherwise there would be no guarantee that it would remain oriented to truth and that it was moving towards truth by way of a process governed by reason. A philosophy which did not proceed in the light of reason according to its own principles and methods would serve little purpose. At the deepest level, the autonomy which philosophy enjoys is rooted in the fact that reason is by its nature oriented to truth and is equipped moreover with the means necessary to arrive at truth.[9]

Catholic teaching does not place faith in some kind of opposition to reason, but rather regards belief and trust in God as a "reasonable" response to the evidence – both the nature of the world around us, and God's self-revelation in Christ, the Scriptures and the Church. Indeed, John Paul II specifically criticises fideism (the belief that faith is independent of reason) for "fail[ing] to recognize the importance of rational knowledge and philosophical discourse for the understanding of faith, indeed for the very possibility of belief in God."[10]

This positive view of reason is by no means confined to Roman Catholicism. Alister McGrath, a leading evangelical Anglican, also argues that reason is trustworthy but limited. Following C.S. Lewis, he seeks to show "the reasonableness of Christianity without imprisoning it within an impersonal and austere rationalism".[11]

Of course, not every Christian is a humanist - both theism and atheism been pressed into the service of profoundly anti-humanist, irrational causes at various points in history. Christians *should* be the first to acknowledge the ways in which their own worldview has been distorted and misused: after all, Christ himself told his followers to take the logs out of their own eyes before criticising the specks in the eyes of their neighbours.[12]

All we are seeking to show is that from the earliest days, some of the most prominent Christian thinkers and teachers have held that reason is a God-given faculty, which (though fallible) is oriented towards the truth. Indeed, the world's largest Christian denomination, with the most systematic body of teaching on the subject, specifically teaches that philosophy has a "valid aspiration to be an *autonomous* enterprise, obeying its own rules and employing the powers of reason alone,"[13] and attacks less humanistic views which "fail to recognise the importance of rational knowledge."

## 3.

The wider credibility of the Christian story is outside the scope of this essay. What is clear is that if the Christian story is true, then there is a credible explanation of the reliability of our capacity for reasoning.

To argue that Christianity can explain the harmony between our faculties for reasoning and the objective reality beyond us is not to set it up as a competitor to evolutionary biology. The relationship between the Christian faith and evolutionary biology is analogous to the relationship between theism and fundamental physics. The existence of a benevolent God is held by Christians (and, indeed, many other theists) to explain the fact the universe appears to be 'fine tuned' to an extraordinary extent, in a way that is hospitable to conscious life.[14] In making this claim, Christians are not offering their position as a rival to physics. Indeed, it is physics that has revealed how finely tuned the universe actually is, and how even tiny changes in some of the most fundamental features of the created order would make it wholly inhospitable to any conscious life at all.

In the area of our rational faculties, the Christian story is likewise intended to complement that offered by evolutionary biology. In neither area is there any suggestion that the scientific theories are wrong, but rather that, when taken in isolation, or 'totalised' as atheistic worldviews, they leave certain characteristics of the world unexplained (in one case, the fact our cognitive capacities track an objective truth, and in the other, the fact that the universe is so fine-tuned in its capacity to sustain life).

When we consider the human capacity for knowledge, three sets of questions need to be asked. They often get confused, and so it is important to distinguish them with some care. The first question asks for the *justification* of our beliefs, the second asks for a *historical explanation* of why humans have come to the kinds of views they have, and the third asks for a *causal explanation* of why humans' cognitive capacities have one particular property, in this case that of (however fallibly) tracking the truth.

Evolutionary biology undoubtedly provides a historical explanation of the development of human beings' rational faculties. And we are surely justified in relying (at least to some extent) on our faculties of reasoning – for they are indispensable to any arguments we can offer. Even in arguing for or against the reliability of reason, we will have to use reason – so we are committed to viewing it as at least partially reliable. However, reason demands that we try and explain things. Even if we are justified in relying on reason, this does not stop us from asking: "Why is it that human beings have developed a capacity to reason in ways that track the truth?"

Philosophers of science have identified two broad categories of explanation. One form of explanation focuses on laws. An event is accounted for by showing that it follows logically from the previous state of the world and what we know to be the laws of nature. Another form of explanation focuses on *ends*. We explain something by showing that a system tends towards a certain end-state, and that an event has happened because it is the best way to achieve that particular end. This latter form of explanation is often called *teleological* explanation (*telos* being the Greek word for 'end').[15]

Evolutionary biology is a form of teleology. It shows why something has happened in terms of the end that is being realised, specifically the survival and replication of the gene or organism or species (depending on your position in a heated debate). It also shows us the mechanism by which the end is realised (namely, mutations and selective pressure). That is part of the appeal and power of evolutionary explanations: they show how natural systems tend towards an end (*telos*) through a process which is not itself intentional.

We use another kind of teleological explanation every time we account for a piece of intentional human behaviour. An event (e.g. my purchase of a suit) is explained by the fact I desire a particular end-state (e.g. getting a new job), and that I believe a certain set of actions need to be taken in order to achieve that (among them, actions which improve my appearance and so impress the interview panel). This kind of explanation shows why an end (*telos*) has been realised through a process which is non-random – the intentions, beliefs and powers of an agent (for this reason, we will refer to it as "intentional explanation").

The Christian claim is that only intentional explanation can adequately account for the existence and character of our universe. As we have stressed already, this is not a form of explanation that seeks to compete with evolutionary biology or the physical sciences. When Christian humanism explains why our faculties of reasoning are reliable, it takes the phenomena described by the sciences (namely, the initial conditions of the universe, the fundamental laws of physics, and the chemical and biological processes by which life, consciousness and the capacity for rational thought emerge) to be the means by which a loving God has chosen to achieve his purposes.

We might say that such explanations are a 'level up' from the scientific ones. They account for features of the world which, we will argue, atheists must regard as vast coincidences. The atheist humanist cannot explain why either (i) the fundamental physical constants in the universe are within the small range that would sustain life or (ii) the faculties generated by the combination of initial conditions, mutations and selective pressures are such as to enable us to get to the truth, in matters of complex reasoning. By contrast, Christian humanism seeks to explain these phenomena by maintaining that the universe is created and sustained by a good and loving God.

Christianity can explain why God values a world in which human beings have faculties of reasoning that are truth-tracking. A benevolent God clearly has reason to value that state of affairs, because (as atheist and Christian humanists would agree) it is objectively good that human beings should come to true rather than false beliefs.

Christian humanism maintains that God is both all-powerful and all-knowing. In consequence, God not only has reason to ensure human beliefs are truth-tracking, but has the capacity to create and sustain a universe in which humans evolve with these properties. This accounts for the way in which the processes of evolution have generated creatures capable of knowing what is objectively true.

As we said at the start of this section, the wider credibility of Christianity is outside the scope of this essay. The twofold argument we are making for is more limited, but still surprising and challenging. The first part of the claim is that Christian humanists have good reason to treat the human capacity for reasoning as (at least to some extent) reliable. We have explained why this is so; and shown that this does not involve any conflict with evolutionary biology. We now turn to the second part of our claim – namely, that it is difficult for atheist humanists to explain why our capacities for reasoning are reliable (truth-directed) as well as useful.[16]

## 4.

Natural selection provides a powerful explanation of why human beings are able to perceive the world around them with some accuracy. Our capacity for sight is a good example. As Richard Dawkins demonstrates, if we assume (i) a process of purely random mutations among the precursors of human beings and (ii) the survival of those precursors with mutations that enhance the animal's capacity for survival and replication, then something as complex and sensitive to the external environment as the human eye can be shown to have been likely to develop in the time it actually did take to evolve.[17]

Could our capacity for reasoning have the same origins? If evolutionary biology can explain the reliability of the organs by which we see and hear, taste and smell, why could a similar explanation not be given for our faculties of reasoning? Surely it is to the advantage of a species – or a sub-group of that species – to be able to reason in ways that tend towards the truth? If that is so, then atheist humanism seems to be sitting on a quite secure branch.

In order to think that reasoning about complex matters – such as philosophy and evolutionary biology – is reliable, we need to think that our ways of thought are not simply "habits of thought" which proved useful for our ancestors' survival and replication, but that there is a harmony between those habits and the correct principles of reasoning.

Reasoning is not simply a matter of applying a straightforward, mathematical formula to the data: as any philosopher of science will tell you, nothing but the truths of mathematics and logic is capable of absolute proof. Reasoning well is a matter of *judging well*. And being able to judge very simple matters which are necessary for humans' survival does not always lead on to being able to judge the complex issues at stake in weighing up the merits of rival scientific theories, or competing philosophical arguments.

Humanists *do* believe that human beings are capable of reasoning well on these complicated matters. Therefore, atheist humanists need to address Walker's challenge: how come we manage to track the truth on issues where *getting things right* is not necessary for survival? After all, it is only in the matters where *getting things right* helps us survive and replicate that evolution can be expected to keep our reasoning on the right tracks.

If we are to trust our reasoning in the complex areas of philosophy and science, we need to explain why we think that – out of the huge number of different ways in which our basic ways of thought could have developed – we have somehow managed to latch on to ways of thought that are true as well as useful. As Walker points out, this is not a question atheist humanists can shrug off. Unless their account of how human beings acquire beliefs explains why we come to true beliefs, then the theory of evolution seems to involve a vast piece of good luck.[18]

As we have seen, Christian humanists have a good answer to this challenge. On the Christian account, a benevolent God has ensured the harmony between the principles of reasoning which seem self-evident to human beings and those which actually yield the truth. But the atheist humanist will find it much more difficult to explain why we have arrived at habits of reasoning that track an objective reality.

> Is it credible that selection for fitness in the prehistoric past should have fixed capacities that are effective in theoretical pursuits that were unimaginable at the time?

Walker is a Christian – and would happily describe himself as a "Christian humanist" – but it is not only religious philosophers who are troubled by this issue. Thomas Nagel's recent book *Mind and Cosmos* echoes much of Walker's argument. He too questions why the specific way in which our ability to reason has developed should track the truth – beyond the most basic levels, at which there is an obvious selective advantage to getting things right. Nagel questions the likelihood that the process of natural selection should have generated creatures with the capacity to discover by reason the truth about a reality that extends vastly beyond the initial appearances – as we take ourselves to have done and to continue to do collectively in science, logic and ethics. He asks: "Is it credible that selection for fitness in the prehistoric past should have fixed capacities that are effective in theoretical pursuits that were unimaginable at the time?"[19]

We will consider the case of ethical truths in a later chapter, but the point which Nagel is making with respect to science and logic has considerable force. The capacities for reasoning which are useful to enable a species to survive and replicate need not also generate truth at this level of complexity. And yet we human beings (who have no choice but to use them) do take our powers of reasoning to have that kind of reliability. The continuing success of our scientific endeavours suggests we are right to do so: but that only shows we are right to have some faith in human reasoning. It does not explain the reliability of reason.

Nagel's answer to this question is (in modern times, at least) a highly unusual one. He argues that there is indeed purpose in the universe, but that this purpose is not personal. This is to say, he believes the harmony between human ways of thinking and objective reality is explained by there being some purpose (*telos*) to which the world is moving. On his account, things happen *because* they are good.

In this sense, though he is not a theist, Nagel's position is far from the atheism of the British Humanist Association. The BHA's "Defining Humanism" web page says that humanism "believes that, in the absence of an afterlife *and any discernible purpose to the universe*, human beings can act to give their own lives meaning by seeking happiness in this life and helping others to do the same"[20] (emphasis added).

Against Nagel's position, explaining things in terms of the goal they seek makes considerably more sense in a universe which is thought to be, in some sense, *designed*. One of the reasons teleological explanations have become less popular since the 17th century is the decline in belief that the world has some wider purpose. Nagel's teleology seems very strange to our minds precisely because it floats free of any wider account of the power or mechanism by which these good things are brought about. We can understand what it means for something to have happened because it realises a good purpose if, and only if, there is a mechanism by which those purposes are brought about. Natural selection provides such an explanation when the "good purpose" is the survival and replication of the species, and intentional explanation provides such an explanation when the "good purpose" is being pursued by an agent. Nagel's account offers neither of these mechanisms – and it doesn't offer us a third alternative.

That undoubted weakness in Nagel's argument in fact strengthens the case being made in this chapter. Nagel cannot be accused of religious "special pleading." No-one can claim that he has been searching for an argument to shore up his religious faith, for he has none. He is forced into some very odd intellectual contortions precisely because he has recognised the depth of the same problem, and the danger that atheistic humanist accounts of evolutionary theory will undermine themselves. He is searching for a way out that is neither Christian humanism nor the kind of atheistic humanism expressed in the Amsterdam Declaration. The implausibility of the middle position he develops only serves to reinforce the case we are making for Christian humanism.

## 5.

To many readers – religious and non-religious alike – our conclusion will seem surprising. Readers used to the message that "faith" and "reason" are opposed, even that Christian faith involves an abandonment of rationality, will find it quite incredible that Christianity could turn out to be the greatest defender of human reason.

If we consider a rather longer historical perspective, however, this conclusion will seem much less surprising. From its very first century the Christian church has taught that the human capacity for reasoning is a gift from God. In doing so, it echoed the far older wisdom literature of the Hebrew Bible. Certainly, Christianity teaches that capacity for reasoning can be distorted by human beings' capacity for wilful self-delusion – for failing to face truths which are not in our own interests, or which disturb our prejudices and preconceptions. But (at least for the vast majority of its teaching throughout the centuries), Christianity has recognised human reason as a God-given faculty which is directed towards the objective truth.

As we have seen in this chapter, Christianity not only values reason, but it offers an explanation of why the human faculties for reasoning help us to track the truth. It is here that Christian humanism seems rather more compelling than its atheist counterpart. As the arguments of Ralph Walker and Thomas Nagel both show, it is very difficult to see why reason should lead us towards truth in a universe which lacks "any discernible purpose." Could it be that Christians are the *best* advocates of humanism's faith in reason?

# chapter 2 – references

1. https://humanism.org.uk/about/humanist-philosophers/faq/whats-so-wrong-with-faith/
2. http://www.mumsnet.com/Talk/mumsnet_live_events/985509-Live-webchat-with-Richard-Dawkins-Wed-23-June-10am-11am?pagingOff=1
3. Ralph Walker at Symposium on 'Philosophy, Evolution and the Human Sciences' at Magdalen College, Oxford on 2 May 2013 (unpublished manuscript).
4. Andrew Brown, 'What is the logic for logical reasoning?' *Guardian* blog on New Insights seminar in Oxford with Ralph Walker (15 May 2013), online at http://www.theguardian.com/commentisfree/andrewbrown/2013/may/15/what-logic-logical-reasoning
5. Jon Elster's *Sour Grapes* and Denise Meyerson's *False Consciousness* are good examples of secular philosophers' engagement with the limitations which self-interest and self-deception places on our capacity to reason well.
6. See, for example, *Second Apology of St Justin Martyr*, 13: 4.
7. See, for example, Peter Harrison, *The Bible, Protestantism, and the Rise of Natural Science* (Cambridge : Cambridge University Press, 1998).
8. See Pope Benedict XVI, General Audience on St Justin, Philosopher and Martyr, 21 March 2007 (Online at http://www.vatican.va/holy_father/benedict_xvi/audiences/2007/documents/hf_ben-xvi_aud_20070321_en.html) and Pope John Paul II, *Faith and Reason* (Catholic Truth Society, 1998), §38.
9. *Faith and Reason*, §49.
10. Ibid., §55.
11. Alister McGrath, *Try seeing it this way: Imagination and reason in the apologetics of C.S. Lewis*, online at http://www.abc.net.au/religion/articles/2013/05/15/3760192.htm
12. Matthew 7.5.
13. *Faith and Reason, §75.*
14. See B. J. Carr and M. Rees, 'The Anthropic Cosmological Principle and the Structure of the Physical World', *Nature* 278 (12 April 1979), pp. 605-12; and R. Collins, 'Evidence for Fine-Tuning', in Neil A. Manson (ed.), *God and Design: The Teleological Argument and Modern Science* (London: Routledge, 2003), pp. 178-99.
15. Charles Taylor, *The Explanation of Behaviour* (London: Routledge & Kegan Paul, 1964), p. 9.
16. In Angus Ritchie's previous report, *From Goodness to God*, he argued only that our capacities for *moral* reasoning caused a problem for atheists. However, the account developed by Ralph Walker shows that this issue also arises for complex theoretical reasoning too.
17. Richard Dawkins, 'Where D'you Get Those Peepers?', *New Statesman and Society*, 16 June 1995, p. 29 and Dan-Erik Nilsson and Susanne Pelger, 'A Pessimistic Estimate of the Time Required for an Eye to Evolve', *Proceedings of the Royal Society of London*, Biological Sciences 256 (1994), pp. 53–8
18. Walker, op. cit.

19  Thomas Nagel, *Mind and Cosmos: Why the Materialist Neo-Darwinian Conception of Nature Is Almost Certainly False*, (Oxford University Press, 2012), 74.
20  https://humanism.org.uk/humanism/

# why dignity?

## 1.

At the heart of 'humanism' is a commitment to the 'human'. This may seem self-evidently true, to the point of being a truism, but what it actually means and why it is a reasonable or justifiable commitment is not so obvious.

Humanists, both religious and atheist, variously talk about the 'dignity' or 'value' or 'worth' or 'sanctity' of human beings, or of human life or of the human 'person'. They often place this commitment at the heart of their ethical thinking (although in different ways) and many seek to establish and secure it legally through a range of specific, named human rights.

The British Humanist Association has as one of its values "recognising the dignity of individuals and treating them with fairness and respect".[1] The *Compendium of Social Teaching of the [Catholic] Church* celebrates "the inviolable dignity of the human person" and says that "a just society can become a reality only when it is based on the respect of the transcendent dignity of the human person".[2] The 1991 IHEU 'Minimum Statement' explained how humanism stands for the building of a "more humane society" through an ethic "based on human and other natural values".[3] The 2002 IHEU Amsterdam Declaration, which has been our guiding light in this essay, affirms the "worth, dignity and autonomy of the individual".

This commitment to human dignity or worth is not a simply theoretical issue, of concern only to moral philosophers. On the contrary, it is central to one of the most famous documents of the 20th century. The Preamble to the Universal Declaration of Human Rights begins by recognising "the inherent dignity and the equal and inalienable rights of all members of the human family" as "the foundation of freedom, justice and peace in the world", and goes on to talk about the "faith" that the peoples of the United Nations have in "the dignity and worth of the human person and in the equal rights of men and women". In this respect, the 1948 Universal Declaration is the perhaps foremost humanistic statement in the modern world.

The Universal Declaration, however, also (famously) fails to justify this faith in human dignity or rather, does so only in negative, historically specific or aspirational terms. Thus, the Preamble declares how "disregard and contempt for human rights have resulted in barbarous acts which have outraged the conscience of mankind", and how "if man is not to be compelled to have recourse, as a last resort, to rebellion against tyranny and oppression, that human rights should be protected by the rule of law." Similarly, it speaks of the "advent" of a world in which "human beings shall enjoy freedom of speech and belief and freedom from fear and want" which has been "proclaimed as the highest aspiration of the common people."

The Preamble's commitment to and justification for human dignity are intelligible but unsatisfying. 'Because we live in the shadow of evil', 'because it is better for all of us if we respect human dignity', 'because we aspire to freedom from fear and want': are of these all admirable but fall short of being philosophically – or ethically – compelling.

This has long been recognised. Jacques Maritain, the prominent Catholic humanist and drafter of the Universal Declaration subsequently remembered that at one of the meetings of a UNESCO National Commission where Human Rights were being discussed,

> someone expressed astonishment that certain champions of violently opposed ideologies had agreed on a list of those rights. 'Yes', they said, 'we agree about the rights but on condition that no one asks us why.'[4]

This seems to have been an unavoidable condition for the Declaration, given what the signatories desired, and some may argue that it still does not matter today. Expedient or aspirational as the Preamble's justifications are, they retain some power even if they don't have authority. Nevertheless, this is still an unhappy condition for humanism to find itself in – having no solid reason why we are committed to the thing (human worth) that we are most committed to. Pragmatic foundations are inherently vulnerable and even if the moral edifice that is constructed above them is unlikely to collapse altogether, it is surely beholden on us to construct it as securely as possible. Indeed, as Christopher McCrudden has noted,

> with the increased political salience of human rights, and the increased use in litigation of human rights language, has come increasing attention on the theoretical underpinnings of human rights.[5]

The edifice may not be about to collapse, but it is having storey upon storey added each year, which makes attention to its foundations all the more essential.

The argument of this chapter is that these commitments to human dignity or worth are better grounded in Christian theism than they are in atheism and, by implication, that unless we pay proper attention to the foundations, the edifice we erect above them is vulnerable, no matter how impressive or ornate it is.

# 2.

Some have claimed that belief in God *devalues* human dignity and undermines human rights. Atheist polemics often depict religion as specifically *anti*-humanist in this regard. 'Religion poisons everything', as the title of Christopher Hitchens' book memorably puts it.

There is a temptation to dismiss such accusations out-of-hand but it is one we should resist as they are far from nonsensical. Christian practice has consistently fallen below the humanising example and teaching of Christ – no surprise there. More alarmingly, Christians have sometimes *justified* their degradation of human dignity with reference to Christianity's founding scriptures.[6] It is, for example, quite possible to cherry pick stories from Old Testament – the conquest of Canaan being the most obvious example – decontextualize them, read them literally, dispense with any theological commentary, and then to use them as evidence of how the call of God can trump any commitment to the human good. These are the kind of arguments that anti-theists have made for centuries but they have done do in part because (some) Christians have given them grounds for doing so.

It is not, therefore, that there aren't the raw materials for anti-humanistic ethics within Christian scripture, nor that Christians haven't over the centuries latched on to such texts as a way of justifying inhumane, un-Christ-like behaviour. This *mea culpa* duly acknowledged, however, it is also right to say that cherry-picking and proof-texting can be used to prove anything, and that only a polemicist blinded by rage would claim this is the full or true picture of the Christian attitude to human dignity. We shall turn in a moment to that fuller picture but, as a placeholder, the words of Human Rights Professor Conor Gearty epitomise the mainstream view of the relationship between Christianity, human dignity and human rights.

> The universal application of these terms [i.e. 'dignity' and 'worth'] in pre-[Universal] Declaration days had been largely associated with progressive elements within religious movements: the Dominican Bartolomé de Las Casas, for example, with his famous 16th-century defence of Native Americans. The Declaration appropriated this language, dispensed with its religious roots and sought to turn it to long-lasting secular effect.[7]

## 3.

Before we can approach the question of how and where Christianity grounds its concept of human dignity, we need first to consider the concept of the 'human'. This is a point to which T.S. Eliot referred in his essay, 'Second thoughts about humanism'. "Humanism", he wrote,

> *Defining the human is difficult when all reference to transcendence – or, at the very least, to any perception of transcendence – is removed.*

depends very heavily…upon the tergiversations of the word 'human' … If you removed from the word 'human' all that the belief in the supernatural has given to man, you can view him finally as no more than an extremely clever, adaptable, and mischievous little animal.[8]

The phrase "all that the belief in the supernatural has given to man" is opaque and open to various interpretations. Eliot's main point, however, is not dependent on those interpretations, namely that defining the human is difficult when all reference to transcendence – or, at the very least, to any perception of transcendence – is removed. This is hardly an exclusively religious point. The evolutionary psychologist Robin Dunbar, coming from as different a position from Eliot as is possible, makes a similar point, in so doing elucidating Eliot's contention:

> As remarkable as our achievements in the arts and sciences may be, it is hard to escape the conclusion that religion is the one phenomenon in which we humans really are different in some qualitative sense from our ape cousins… We should not, in our haste, overlook the important role religion has played in human affairs, helping to bond communities and so enabling them to meet the challenges that the planet has thrown at them. Even today, its contribution to human psychological wellbeing is probably sufficient to raise serious questions about whether the human race could do without it.[9]

This offers an entirely functional understanding of religion, in which it is a unique human endeavour but one that is evolutionarily driven and determined rather than in any way a response to reality. This (significant) difference aside, however, the point stands: if you seek an idea of the human on which to ground ideas of human dignity and rights, discarding the ideas and practices associated with religion leaves the boundaries blurred. Without some concept of self-transcendence – note: not agreement about it but simply acknowledging the concept – it is hard to see why one should draw the lines of the human to exclude, say, higher primates.

This may be turned around and put another way. If the criteria for humanity are based on cognitive or emotional faculties, there is no good reason to exclude certain other primates, like chimpanzees, orang-utans, and gorillas, and possibly even other animals such as dolphins, from the category of 'human' and (much of) what goes with it. This is precisely what some, like those involved in the Great Ape Project have argued, urging a UN Declaration of the Rights of Great Apes that would ensure chimpanzees, bonobos, gorillas and orang-utans should be recognised as having rights to life, liberty and freedom from torture.

While many people agree that such higher primates should be protected in these ways, they are uneasy about categorising them as quasi-human simply on account of their cognitive faculties. If they are just uneasy about this, however, the obverse of the same argument – that just as some great apes do fall into the category of human, some people don't – fully revolts them. By this reasoning, a healthy adult chimpanzee is more 'human', and has a greater call on our moral duty, than, say, a severely physically or mentally handicapped child.

If we dispense with any concept of (Eliot's) "supernatural", or (Dunbar's) "religion" or (Catholic Social Teaching's) "openness to transcendence" and choose instead cognitive capacity as the mark and measure of 'humanity', it is clear that there are some living *Homo sapiens* who do not exhibit, and will never develop, that capacity. It follows that their dignity (and their rights) is accordingly limited and is certainly less than that of certain primate cousins who have and make use of their higher cognitive faculties.

This is a highly complex – and highly contentious – debate which need not be resolved for the sake of the argument we are pursuing in this chapter. Rather, it is raised simply to illustrate that the question of the boundaries of the human are neither straightforward nor simply theoretical. How one understands what demarcates and distinguishes the 'human' is not obvious, and where one draws the line of "humanity" cannot but affect how one treats those examples that fall on either side.

## 4.

If the category of human is neither obvious nor natural, ascribing dignity or worth to *each and every* individual who falls within that category is even less natural.

This is emphatically not to say that humans don't have great capacity for goodness, for solidarity, for hospitality, and for generosity: in short, for behaving with dignity and affirming the worth of others. Nor is it to claim that we direct those virtues solely towards kin and kith, to those to whom we are related, whom we know, or from whom we may get some advantage. Humans are capable of enormous goodness to strangers just as to friends.

What it is to say is that, however generous we *can* be, it is certainly not natural or obvious for humans to ascribe dignity and worth to *all* humans *everywhere, irrespective* of capacity or circumstance. The most cursory reading of human history confirms this, and the West is certainly no different to anywhere else in this respect. In the second century, the Roman jurist Gaius explained how he could rely on three tests to establish a person's status – were they free or unfree? were they a citizen or foreign born? were they a paterfamilias or in the power of an ancestor? These were enough to tell not simply where someone stood in the social pecking order but, more substantially, whether they were worth anything at all. Slaves could hold high office but were still effectively non-persons. Women were similarly restricted, their status and worth dependent entirely on the men in their lives. Roman law was limited to relations "between men who shared in the worship of the city, sacrificing at the same altars. They alone were citizens".[10] Much the same judgement was made in every empire of the ancient world. It was the intrusion of Christianity, and in particular its historically unusual concept of universal human worth, into the thought world of late antiquity that changed this.

To understand this it is important first to ask what it means to say that something has worth. The instinctive response to this is to seek the answer in a particular capacity or quality or function of the thing under discussion. A house has worth because of its size, style and location; a car because of its design and performance; a meal because of its taste and artistry; and so forth. However, it soon becomes clear that this is a limiting approach. A child's teddy bear, for example, may be badly made, torn and battered beyond all recognition, incapable of *doing* anything, and with a 'functionality' of precisely zero, and yet have immense and incommensurable worth. A love letter or family photograph may be similarly damaged and scruffy but have a similar value. By contrast, a brand new consumer product – a Tablet or an iPhone 6 say – may have astonishingly impressive functionality but be so cosmetically damaged to as make it all but worthless. The properties or capacities of an object are no sure guide to its worth.

In his *Utopia*, Thomas More describes how the Utopians favour this view, valuing things in proportion to their usefulness, in contrast to our (more absurd) practice of valuing things on account of their scarcity. Thus, the Utopians value iron, which is plentiful but useful, over gold and silver, which are rare and useless. This idea of 'value through scarcity' is indeed a popular alternative to the idea of 'value through use' but it faces similar problems.

It is certainly true, for example, the that price of gold rises or falls according to its availability (among other factors) but this indicates nothing more than the fact the people do value rare things; not that rarity itself is inherently valuable. The *Codex Sinaiticus* and the Lindesfarne Gospels are unique manuscripts and of enormous value. However, the early drafts of this essay and the fly tip at the end of my road are both similarly unique – there is nothing else quite like it in the whole the world – but they pretty much worthless. A thing is not necessarily valuable simply because it is scarce or even unique.

The criterion for the worth of a thing is not, therefore, what it can do, what it looks like, or how many of them there are in existence. Rather, the primary criterion for worth is simply whether someone values it. The child's teddy bear, the love letter, and the family photograph have value because the child, lover or mother is profoundly attached to them. The *Codex Sinaiaticus* and the Lindesfarne Gospels have similar worth because scholars (and Christians) around the world value them for what they reveals about early Christianity. The damaged iPhone 6 or the fly tip are all but worthless because no-one values them. Disconcerting and relativistic as it may seem, the worth of something is dependent on the judgment of a person.

There is, of course, a difference between worth and dignity. A thing may have worth but it makes no sense to say that it has dignity. Dignity is an epithet we attach only to humans and the things they do. However, to say that a human has dignity is to presuppose that he or she also has worth. It is this understanding of worth – someone has worth because they are valued by another – that lies at the heart of the Christian understanding of human dignity, the 'another' in this context being, of course, God.

# 5.

The biblical foundations of human dignity are well known, and although there are a number that might be cited, two are critical.[11] The first is that all humans are made in the image of God and the second is that Christ died for all.

There have been innumerable attempts to define what being made in the image of God 'means', some more successful than others. For a time in the post-Reformation period, rationality was deemed to be *the* distinctive and decisive human capacity and therefore the mark of God's image. This had little textual warrant, however, and is largely discarded by theologians today. In its place, a number of other definitions and characteristics stand out.

First, there is the 'substantive' definition: being made in the image of God means sharing some of his substantial characteristics, not so much rationality as creativity, productivity and generosity. The God in whose image humans are made is a creative, productive and generous God.

Second, there is the 'functional' definition: being made in the image of God means we have a particular job to do, a job that is variously defined as "ruling over", "subdu[ing]", "work[ing]…and tak[ing] care of" and "nam[ing]" creation, or alternatively of "stewardship".

Finally, there is the relational definition: being made in the image of God means existing in relationship to him, to other humans and to the rest of creation in a way that reflects something of God's own relational nature.

These are all defensible definitions but demand careful handling. They outline, in effect, a normative picture of the human in the sense of what humans *should ideally be like*. Alone of all creatures, we have a nature capable of loving, of sacrificial relationship with God and one other; qualities including, but not limited to, creativity, productivity and generosity; and the duty to rule and steward the rest of creation. Between them, these elements constitute the normative definition of human.

Crucially, however, this is an ideal picture, outlining what humans *should* be like, not what they *are* like. Our humanity may be distinguished by and aspire to this picture, but it consistently fails to achieve it. Recognising this is important. Were we to predicate human worth on such nature, behaviour or capacities – on our relationality, our productivity, our generosity, etc. – our consistent failure to live up to these standards would erode that worth. In short, it would be a way of showing not human worth but worthlessness.

> *Humans are not creatures that are valued by God because they bear the imago dei. Humans are creatures that bear the imago dei because they valued by God.*

This is not, however, how Christian scripture and thought does describe human worth. Indeed, the biblical understanding of the image of God is not interested in parsing the term, still less judging human worth by the extent to which we fulfil its constituent elements. Humans are not creatures that are valued by God because they bear the *imago dei*. Humans are creatures that bear the *imago dei* because they are valued by God.

Psalm 8 offers an illustration of this. It is a short but powerful meditation on human nature in the light of the image. The beings exalted in the song are recognisably those of the creation story "a little lower than the angels and crowned…with glory and honour… rulers over the works of your hands". And yet, in spite of this, the Psalmist is still astonished that God should care for humans:

When I consider your heavens,
>    the work of your fingers,
> the moon and the stars,
>    which you have set in place,
> what is mankind that you are mindful of them,
>    human beings that you care for them?"

Humans are indeed impressive and exalted beings. But they are loved by God irrespective of those qualities.

A similar point can be made from the New Testament. Humanity in the light of Christ is a reformed humanity, being transformed into his image, exhorted to put on their new selves "created to be like God in true righteousness and holiness."[12] Yet, as in the Old Testament, humanity's value is not predicated on our bearing the "image of Christ" or wearing that "new self". On the contrary, as with Psalm 8, St. Paul in particular is clear that it was nothing that humans did that merited God's attention in Christ. Like the Psalmist, he is incredulous that God is mindful of humans and should care for them as profoundly as he does. Our worth is not depended on our merits. It is not predicated on our exercising the image of God in us but of God loving those creatures who bear that image.

> This worth is entirely a divine ascription, not tied to our purported capacities, not tied to anything 'inherent' or achieved by human beings, but rooted in God's relationship to humanity, his decisions, declarations, and commands towards us.[13]

# 6.

This has obvious implications for how we should treat one another. Every person is made in the image of God; made in order to be in relationship, to be loving, creative, generous, and so forth. Every person fails in this commission. Some fail through ignorance, some through weakness, some through their own deliberate fault, and some through no fault of their own or anyone else. This is what is meant when Paul says all have sinned and fallen short of the glory of God: not the self-flagellating miserabilism of caricature but a recognition that all of us fail to be as loving and faithful, forgiving and forbearing, gentle and generous, as we should. In short, that we don't live up to the image of God.

> *Human worth is dependent not on how loving they are but how loved they are.*

However, our worth is not contingent on us doing so. Human worth or dignity is not dependent on our being generous or relational or responsible, any more than it is dependent on more obviously cognitive capacities, such as our being capable of rational thought or free choice. Human worth is dependent not on how loving they are but how loved they are. In the long-run it appears that the image of the child's battered teddy bear, while misleading in so many small ways, is right in one big one: it is not our capacities or beauty or lack thereof that matters; it is how much we are loved.

This is profoundly important for how we treat one another. For, if all the above is true, whenever I interact with another creature that bears the image of God, I am interacting with someone who is loved fully and permanently by God. In Rowan Williams' words,

> what I recognize in recognizing the dignity of the other is that they have a standing before God, which is, of its nature, invulnerable to the success or failure of any other relationship or any situation in the contingent world.[14]

Their capacities and moral qualities, while being relevant to their role in society, have no bearing on their worth, which is determined by God alone.

This helps explain why the incursion of Christian ethical commitments into the ancient world was so strange, even incomprehensible, to so many. Early Christians repeatedly drew attention to the universality and impartiality of God's – and, in theory, therefore their – love. "Persons of every age are treated by us with respect…We do not test them by their looks, nor do we judge of those who come to us by their outward appearance," explained the Syrian writer Tatian.[15] *All* humans were to be respected, irrespective of their circumstance or status, because God had made *all* in his own image, and Christ had given himself for all. The fact that he had come as a servant, without the trappings of power or status, reinforced this ethic.

Words are one thing, of course; actions another. There was inevitably a touch of polemic to some Christian claims. The church's funds are not "spent on feasts, and drinking bouts, and eating houses," (unlike those of pagan religions) explained the theologian Tertullian.[16] Instead, they were used "to support and bury poor people, to supply the wants of boys and girls destitute of means and parents, and of old persons confined to the house". Yet, this activity is too widely testified, not least by those who were Christianity's enemies, to be incredible. When the last pagan emperor, Julian the Apostate, complained how "the impious Galileans" (as he called them) "support our poor in addition to their own"[17] he confirmed what Tertuillian, and others, claimed.

The clearest mark of the early church's humanism was found not just in its support of the pagan poor but in the attention and respect it paid to those on the very margins of life.

The church inherited the – to the ancient world unfathomable – Jewish prohibition on abortion and infanticide.[18] "[We] regard the foetus in the womb as a created being, and therefore an object of God's care," wrote Athenagoras.[19] "Exposing" new-born children – effectively leaving them to die – wrote Justin Martyr in his *First Apology*, "is the part of wicked men," something to be avoided "lest we should sin against God".[20] Children, within and without the womb, were no less loved by God than the hungry poor or the powerful rich.

The church's attitude to the other group of marginal humans, slaves, was more ambiguous, if only slightly more so. Because slavery ranged from comfortable domestic employment to brutal enslavement in the ancient world, the initial Christian response was to ameliorate rather than abolish it. Paul tried to humanise master-slave relations, whilst dropping hints about manumission. The early Epistle of Barnabas instructed masters not to "issue orders with bitterness to your maidservant or your manservant, who trust in the same God, lest you should not reverence that God who is above both."[21] It was the "trust in the same God" that proved decisive in the long run. The very fact the slaves and masters shared the same body of Christ in the Eucharist slowly undermined the inherent inequality of the master-slave relationship. In time this would underpin Gregory of Nyssa's unequivocal and indignant denunciation of slavery in his fourth sermon on the book of Ecclesiastes in 379 and, eventually, lead to the erosion of the institution in later centuries.[22]

Such attitudes to the poor, the unborn, the new-born and slaves were eccentric. More directly challenging was the Christian attitude to taking life. Christians exhibited a distinct reluctance to take human lives. They denounced the public exhibition of the arena and rejected even the authorised killing of an army. No Christian served in imperial armies until about 170 AD and even afterwards doing so was treated with great suspicion.[23] "How will a Christian man war, nay, how will he serve even in peace, without a sword, which the Lord has taken away?" asked the incredulous Tertullian.[24] Hippolytus of Rome was even stronger. "Any catechumen or believer who wishes to become a soldier must be dismissed from the church because they have despised God."[25] Some went further still and questioned even judicial killing. "We cannot endure even to see a man put to death, though justly", wrote Athenagoras in his *Plea for the Christians*.[26]

Altogether, for all its undoubted hesitations and failures – not that modern Western Christian authors are in any position to cast stones – the early Christian church exhibited a deep and empire-transforming ideological and practical commitment to the dignity and worth of the human. This was a powerful and determined humanism, which may have been repeatedly betrayed in the time of Christendom, but was never altogether lost.

This humanism was rooted in the distinct Christian belief that God loved each and every human he created and redeemed, and that therefore, in the words of Lactantius, "it is always unlawful to put to death a man, [because] God willed [him] to be a sacred animal."[27]

# 7.

This commitment to human dignity underpins humanism today. The human being is of worth irrespective of his or her standing in society, employment, or judgement by any other cultural norm.

However, this is the juncture at which the vulnerability of non-Christian humanist commitment to ineradicable human dignity becomes clear, for the simple reason that the foundational reason behind the Christian humanist commitment to human dignity is not available to atheists. Quite clearly it makes no sense for an atheist to say that God loves all those who bear his image, irrespective of whether they or anyone else erases, or even acknowledges, that image. The non-Christian humanist commitment to ineradicable human dignity must rely on some other factor and none of these are quite up to the job.

Two attempts stand out. Best known is the argument from capacities associated originally with Immanuel Kant. The argument here is that humans (uniquely) have the capacity for rational agency, and that it is this capacity to direct their will to their own freely-chosen ends which means that "man exists as an end in himself, [and] not merely as a means for arbitrary use by this or that will."[28] "Anything possessing the capacity to set ends and act according to reason is an end in itself, however well or badly it may exercise the capacity."[29] Since it is rational nature that makes you a person, it is in respecting your rational nature that another pays proper respect to you.[30]

This sounds reasonable and humane but it is beset with problems. First, there is the problem of relative worth. As Nicholas Wolterstorff has observed, "if possessing the capacity for rational action gives worth to a human being, how can it be that possessing that capacity to a greater degree does not give a human being greater worth?"[31] If rational capacity can be equated to worth, are not those who are apparently more rational not also worth more?

Irrespective of the answer to this question, a second problem, pertaining to the other end of the spectrum is rather more alarming. What of those human beings that do not have rational capacity? There are many: infants, the mentally disabled, those with degenerative conditions. Do they therefore not have worth or dignity?

In some instances, the basic criterion of 'rational capacity' can be massaged to accommodate them. Infants, for example, do not have rational capacity but so long as human dignity is deemed to rest not on possession of rationality but *potential* possession of rationality, it can be argued that they do in fact have dignity and worth.

But this argument does not work for those with permanent mental illness or with degenerative conditions, like Alzheimer's or dementia, who have either never possessed such rationality, or have lost it and have no chance to acquiring it again. In these instances, there is no potential possession of rationality and so, presumably, no dignity and worth.

In respect of this, the 'rational capacities' basis for humanism faces an attendant problem, to which we alluded earlier, namely how one defines the category of 'human' and how far one therefore extends the protection. There can be no doubt that certain non-human animals, like chimpanzees, have capacity for rational agency. According to the logic of 'rational capacities', 'human' dignity and worth must therefore be extended to them.

It is, of course, possible that people will agree that it is perfectly right to accord some (all?) higher primates a degree of respect and dignity by dint of their cognitive and rational faculties. However, the logic of the 'rational faculties' approach also demands that those *Homo sapiens*, such as cerebrally-impaired infants or elderly people with advanced dementia, who do not have rational faculties thereby slip out of the human category and lose the dignity (and protection) that affords. By such reasoning, the UN Convention on the rights of persons with disabilities is unsustainable. As Conor Gearty has observed, such a convention is certainly not something that Kant or Hobbes would have contemplated.[32]

The idea of basing humanism on 'rational capacity' is, therefore, flawed and vulnerable. More worryingly, it threatens to tilt the definition of human, with all its implications for worth, dignity and social protection, towards the more rational, the more independent, the more articulate in society – precisely to those who are in a position of strength in a liberal society that prides itself on individualism, autonomy and rational debate. Without intending to, even with the best of intentions, atheistic humanism of this kind ends up undermining precisely the commitment to universal, equal human dignity that is supposed to mark humanism.

# 8.

The second response to the need for non-theistic foundations for human dignity is to assert that one does not need any allegedly external or objective basis, such as being loved by God or having rational faculties, in order to recognise human dignity. Rather, simply believing that humans have dignity is enough.

This is the idea of the 'useful myth', the commitment which, if sufficiently widely held, becomes as close to being an objective fact as is possible for humans to achieve in such circumstances. This may sound absurd – a hauling oneself up by one's ethical bootstraps – but it is effectively the means by which the UN Declaration of Human Rights has existed over the last 65 years. The success of this approach – with an attitude of "we agree about the rights but on condition that no one asks us why" – has been far from negligible.

However, the example of the UN Declaration illustrates precisely the problem with this approach. Put simply, it works when it works. In countries and cultures that sign up to, and mentally internalise the Declaration, it retains a genuine power that becomes, in effect, authority. However, in times and places that fail to recognise, let alone internalise the ideas, it has no hold. It is, in effect, a kind of faith. If held with sufficient strength and confidence, it can discipline other less benevolent attitudes to the human. If not, it has no power at all.

It is perhaps for this reason that adherents of human rights sometimes attack its critics with such vigour. On this understanding, to criticise human rights is not to disagree about a political structure or even an ethical system, but to risk revealing the subjective basis of the whole system, to show that its foundation is no stronger than a silent, collective act of will. It is the equivalent of the Reformers casting doubts on what the priest accomplishes during Mass.

Thus, while this approach *can* ground humanism's commitment to equal and inalienable human dignity, it depends on everyone believing in it, in a colossal act of communal faith. This has worked well enough in the Western world for last two generations but its success beyond these (historically Christian) countries has been far less impressive. It is clearly too philosophically vulnerable an approach to sustain this commitment in the long run.

# 9.

To conclude: this chapter has emphatically not argued that atheist humanists have any less commitment to human dignity than Christian humanists. Indeed, regrettably (for Christians at least) it is atheist humanists who have sometimes lead the way in securing human dignity around the world over the last half century. In this respect, Christians have much to learn from them.

Nor has it pretended that the seeds of anti-humanist behaviour are entirely absent in the Christian scriptures. Read in the wrong way by the wrong person with the wrong motives the Bible, or bits of it, can be used to justify manifestly anti-humanist behaviour.

What it *has* argued is that when the Bible has been properly read – meaning within the mainstream tradition – Christian beliefs have underpinned a commitment to human dignity. This is a commitment that transformed the ancient world and bequeathed to the modern one the idea, albeit battered and bruised by Christendom, that all humans are possessed of an equal, permanent, incommensurable worth.

This worth is predicated on Christian ideas, supremely that of the image of God and the sacrifice of Christ. Without it, we have argued, humanism's commitment to human dignity is weaker and ultimately unsustainable. None of the alternatives offered – human dignity based on our cognitive or rational faculties, or human dignity based on a collective act of will – is sufficiently robust. Without Christianity, this plank of humanism – perhaps the most important we have discussed in this essay – is in danger of decay.

A final word: few sane people, and certainly not the authors of this essay, imagine that this decay is imminent or severe. The "without Christianity we will plunge back into the nightmares of the Gulag" argument is a canard. However, when respected ethicists make serious arguments about the non-human status of mentally-disabled infants;[33] medical ethicists make sincere case for infanticide (or post-natal termination as they euphemistically call it);[34] and advanced Western democracies legislate for the euthanasia of children, one can see the thread of equal, permanent, incommensurable dignity for all humans fraying.

## chapter 3 – references

1. https://humanism.org.uk/about/our-values/
2. #107, #132
3. The Minimum Statement is a little opaque here. Competitiveness and belligerence are, after all, thoroughly "human" and "natural" traits that have been and are deeply valued by certain individuals and cultures, but it is doubtful that they could play any significant role in building a humane society.
4. Jacques Maritain, 'Introduction', in *Human Rights: Comments and Interpretations*, symposium edited by UNESCO (New York, Columbia University Press, 1949); http://unesdoc.unesco.org/images/0015/001550/155042eb.pdf
5. Christopher McCrudden, 'In Pursuit of Human Dignity: An Introduction to Current Debates', in *Understanding Human Dignity*, (ed.) Christopher McCrudden (Oxford : Oxford University Press, 2013), p. 2.
6. An example here would be the various biblical justifications for the slave trade and slavery more generally. See Nick Spencer, *Freedom and Order: History, Politics and the English Bible* (Hodder and Stoughton, 2012), pp. 170-75.
7. Conor Gearty, 'Something to Declare', *Rationalist Association*, 5 November 2008; http://rationalist.org.uk/articles/1901/something-to-declare
8. Eliot, *Selected Essays*, p. 485.
9. Robin Dunbar, *The Human Story* (Faber and Faber, 2004), pp. 197-199.
10. Larry Siedentop, *Inventing the Individual: The Origins of Western Liberalism* (Allen Lane, 2014), p. 24.
11. See David P. Gusshe, *The Sacredness of Human Life: Why an Ancient Biblical Vision Is Key to the World's Future* (Wm. B. Eerdmans Publishing Company, 2013).
12. Ephesians 4.24.
13. See Gusshe, *Sacredness*, p. 114.
14. Rowan Williams, *Faith in the Public Square* (Bloomsbury, 2012), p. 171.
15. 'To the Greeks', in *The Ante-Nicene fathers: translations of the writings of the fathers down to A.D. 325*, (eds.) Alexander Roberts and James Donaldson, (Grand Rapids : Eerdmans, 1979-1986), Vol. 2, p. 78.
16. 'Apology', in *Ante-Nicene Fathers*, 3:46.
17. Letter to Arsacius, quoted in *The Roman World: Sources And Interpretation* (ed.) D. Brendan Nagle (Pearson/Prentice Hall, 2005), p. 269.
18. See Michael J. Gorman, *Abortion and the Early Church: Christian, Jewish, and Pagan Attitudes in the Greco-Roman World* (1998).
19. 'A Plea for the Christians', in *Ante-Nicene Fathers*, 2:147.
20. 'First Apology', in *Ante-Nicene Fathers*, 1:172.

21  *Ante-Nicene Fathers*, 1:148.
22  David Bentley Hart, *Atheist Delusions: The Christian Revolution and its Fashionable Enemies* (Yale, 2009), pp. 177-79. See also, Siedentop, *Inventing the Individual*
23  Frances M. Young. "The Early Church: Military Service, War and Peace" *Theology*, 92, no. 750 (November 1, 1989); Kirk R. MacGregor, "Nonviolence in the Ancient Church and Christian Obedience", *Themelios*, 33, no. 1, (2008): 16-17.
24  'On Idolatry', in *Ante-Nicene Fathers*, 3:73.
25  *The Apostolic Tradition*, 16.17-19.
26  'A Plea for the Christians', in *Ante-Nicene Fathers*, 2:147.
27  'Divine Institutes Vol VI', in *Ante-Nicene Fathers*, 7:187.
28  Quoted in Gusshe, *Sacredness*, p. 252.
29  Nicholas Wolterstorff, *Justice: Rights and Wrongs* (Princeton, N.J.: Princeton University Press, 2008), p. 327, quoting Wood XXXX.
30  Wolterstorff, *Justice*, p. 329, quoting Allen Wood, *Kant's Ethical Thought* (Cambridge: Cambridge University Press, 1999), p. 121.
31  Wolterstorff, *Justice*, p. 327.
32  http://www.un.org/disabilities/convention/conventionfull.shtml ; Conor Gearty, 'Something to Declare', op. cit.
33  See, for example, Peter Singer, *Rethinking Life & Death: The Collapse of Our Traditional Ethics* (Oxford : Oxford University Press, 1995).
34  Alberto Giubilini & Francesca Minerva, 'After-birth abortion: why should the baby live?' Journal of Medical Ethics, February 2012: http://jme.bmj.com/content/early/2012/03/01/medethics-2011-100411.full

# 4

# why morality?

## 1.

The very first statement of the Amsterdam Declaration is that "humanism is ethical", which the Declaration expands on in two ways.

Firstly, it tells us that humanism "affirms the worth, dignity and autonomy of the individual and the right of every human being to the greatest possible freedom compatible with the rights of others." We considered this issue in the previous chapter, and explained why we believe Christianity – with its doctrines of the image of God and the sacrifice of Christ – provides the most robust foundation for this commitment.

Second, the Declaration tells us that humanists believe morality is "an intrinsic part of human nature based on understanding and a concern for others, needing no external sanction."

It is this second claim aspect – the *nature* of morality – that we will examine in this chapter. Christian and atheist humanists both take ethics extremely seriously. In particular, they take rational reflection to be a very important part of ethics: using our reasoning to strip away prejudice and outmoded ways of thinking, so that we make the right judgements about how to treat each other, how to build a just and generous community, and how to care for the planet and for generations as yet unborn.

In this chapter, we will ask what the nature of ethics is, and why we should be confident human beings can come to accurate ethical judgments by means of their reasoning and empathy. This draws some of the threads of the last two chapters together, as it will lead us back to the question of why we trust reason as a reliable tool for getting to the truth. But before we get onto the reliability (or otherwise) of our ethical judgments, we need to ask what kind of thing ethics is in the first place.

One point of terminology here: as the Cambridge Dictionary of Philosophy notes, "ethics" is "commonly used interchangeably with 'morality'" but is also sometimes used "more narrowly to mean the moral principles of a particular tradition, group or individual."[1] In this context, we will be following the more generous usage, and taking 'ethics' and 'morality' to refer to the wide subject of what is truly good, right and/or valuable, and how this should guide our attitudes and behaviour as human beings.

## 2.

Let us first consider what kind of thing ethical truth might be. Humanists believe it *matters*, and that it *should guide our actions*. It must surely then, in some sense, be *objective*. Morality is not whatever I want it to be. There are a range of statements in the Amsterdam Declaration which make this very clear: from its talk of the "worth, dignity and autonomy" of the individual, and the range of "rights" it asserts that human beings have.

The Declaration is full of ethical imperatives: humans have a *right* to "the greatest possible freedom compatible with the rights of others," "democracy and human development are matters of *right*," "the application of science and technology *must* be tempered by human values." It says that humanists have a *"duty* of care to all of humanity including future generations". (All emphases in quotations are added). What is the source of these imperatives? What kind of thing are they, if not simply expressions of taste or fashion which we can change?

The Declaration is silent on this, except to say one vague and positive thing (that morality is "an intrinsic part of human nature") and one very specific and negative thing (that it "need[s] no external sanction.")

We suspect that the negative point here is partly aimed at religious people. Maybe there is an implicit contrast here between the rather selfish motives of some religious people (who need the promise of heaven or the threat of hell to motivate their good deeds) with the selflessness of atheistic humanism (in which good deeds are seen as ends in themselves). If so, we ought to concede that atheist humanists have a point: religious people (including, no doubt, some Christian humanists) do sometimes fall into the trap of believing that eternal rewards are the reason to do the right thing. And if that is really the motivation for Christian action – "I do the right thing because it will win me eternal bliss" – then it is little or no better than the most self-centred form of atheism. The Christian who is motivated in this way is just as thoroughly selfish, only with a different set of beliefs about what maximises their self-interest.

To commend Christian ethics on the basis of eternal rewards is, however, to miss the point: for the Christian understanding is that love is the supreme standard of ethics. This flows from the Christian conviction that God himself *is* love; that there is communion and sharing at the very heart of the divine. This returns us to the two key Christian doctrines we laid out in the previous chapter – that human beings are made in the image of God (a

God whom Christianity claims has relationship at his heart) and that God is revealed to us most fully in the self-sacrifice of Christ. Thus, a truly Christian ethics is not a matter of God deciding arbitrarily what to declare "good" or "bad." Rather, as the nature of God, revealed in Jesus Christ, is self-giving love, it is that kind of love which is of ultimate value.

The primary motivation for Christians to love in this way is not the fear of damnation or the prospect of eternal bliss. The three central motivations for the Christian to love are: firstly, appreciation of the sheer *goodness* of this love (that is to say, a recognition that such love is *intrinsically* good, not simply good because God has declared it to be so); second, recognition that, as human beings were created for such love, it is in this love that we will alone find fulfilment (as St Augustine writes "our hearts are restless, until they find their rest in you");[2] and, third, a sense of gratitude that God has offered himself for us in Jesus Christ (as the New Testament expresses it, "We love because God first loved us").[3]

Pope Benedict XVI expanded on this in his encyclical *Deus caritas est* (God is love):

> Love of God and love of neighbour are thus inseparable, they form a single commandment. But both live from the love of God who has loved us first. No longer is it a question, then, of a "commandment" imposed from without and calling for the impossible, but rather of a freely-bestowed experience of love from within, a love which by its very nature must then be shared with others. Love grows through love. Love is "divine" because it comes from God and unites us to God; through this unifying process it makes us a "we" which transcends our divisions and makes us one, until in the end God is "all in all."[4]

The Christian humanist, then, shares with the atheist humanist a conception of ethics as an *imperative:* both believe that as human beings we are called to behave in certain ways, independent of our current feelings or preferences. What is distinctive about Christian humanism is its understanding of the way humans are best motivated to grow and flourish. The Christian understanding of how human beings are transformed is centred on God's self-sacrifice and grace. It could not be further from the common parody of religious morality as a matter of arbitrarily issued divine commands which are to be obeyed out of a mixture of fear and calculation. Christians must, however, recognise the many examples of bad teaching on this subject within our community which live up to the parody, and do not communicate the reality of the faith.

# 3.

What does atheist humanism have to say about the nature of ethical imperatives? This is a subject on which humanist philosophers admit to substantial disagreement.[5]

Atheist humanists vary in their metaphysics – from those who take ethical truth to be every bit as objective as scientific truth, through to those who take ethical truth to be an expression of the sensibilities and sentiments of human beings.

We will call the first group 'moral realists.' For the sake of conceptual clarity, we will offer a brief definition of this term. In the rest of this chapter, we use 'moral realism' to denote the conviction that there are objectively right and wrong answers to questions like 'How ought human beings to behave in specified circumstances?' and 'What states of affairs, activities or character traits are valuable and worthy of pursuit?' (To philosophers, this formulation may seem too vague, most notably the meaning of 'objective,' so we offer a more technical definition in the footnotes.)[6]

Sam Harris is a very clear example of an atheist humanist who is also a moral realist. He writes that:

> [T]here are right and wrong answers to moral questions, just as there are right and wrong answers to questions of physics, and such answers may one day fall within reach of the maturing sciences of mind.[7]

This sounds like a fairly straightforward assertion of moral realism. He writes that, given

> there are facts – real facts – to be known about how conscious beings can experience the worst possible misery and the greatest possible well-being, it is objectively true to say that there are right and wrong answers to moral questions.[8]

A.C. Grayling offers a similar, account of moral truth. He rejects the "transcendentalism" of the Judaeo-Christian tradition, on which "man's good lies in submission to an external authority," but he does affirm

> the fundamental idea ... that people possess reason, and that by using it they can choose lives worth living for themselves and respectful of their fellows ... In humanist ethics the individual is responsible for achieving the good as a free member of a community of free agents [whereas] in religious ethics he achieves the good by obedience to an authority which tells him what his goals are and how he should live.[9]

Grayling takes there to be better and worse answers to the questions of what lives are worth living, and in which ways we ought to be respectful of our fellows. He regards "the arms trade, poverty in the Third World, the continuance of slavery under many guises and names ... [and] the ethical challenge posed by environmental problems caused by the heedless and insatiable rush for economic growth everywhere" – as well, of course, as the "antipathies and conflicts" generated by religion – as among the most important and urgent moral issues of our time.[10]

On the definition of 'moral realism' being used in this essay, both of these humanist philosophers qualify as moral realists. Both take the question 'how ought I to live?' to have better or worse answers, which amount to more than statements of what is in my self-interest. For both, moral truth is discerned not invented.

## 4.

If moral truth is discovered, rather than invented, then the question we raised in chapter two rears its head again. How are human beings capable of discerning moral truths?[11]

In many ways this is a more acute problem than that outlined earlier in the essay. Even if you didn't think there was a general issue with the reliability of human reason, there are problems specific to moral reasoning. In the case of morality, we have good reason to believe that what is *selectively advantageous* and what is *right* differ. If our only explanation of the reliability of our rational faculties goes via natural selection (in an otherwise purposeless universe), we have a problem – for, as we argued at some length in Chapter Two, natural selection only explains why our cognitive faculties are useful, not why they are reliable.

Are those the only two alternatives – or is there some third explanation available in the case of moral knowledge? Perhaps moral codes evolve to encourage us to co-operate, and thus to promote collective well-being more effectively. There is both an obvious selective advantage to this and a strong case for thinking the fruits of such co-operation are objectively good – so this looks like a way of explaining both the usefulness and the reliability of our moral beliefs. This position has been advanced by Sam Harris, both in a range of popular philosophical books, and in public lectures sponsored by the British Humanist Association. For this reason, we will focus on his arguments – as a prominent, mainstream atheist humanist position that looks well-equipped to answer the problem we have identified.

Sam Harris argues it is self-evident that human "well-being" is objectively valuable. Indeed, he argues that well-being is the only genuine moral value, all other candidates being relics of religion or other forms of superstition. Harris takes his position to reconcile the objectivity of morality with the need to explain how humans, as products of the process of natural selection, might come to be able to grasp moral truths. He argues that a moment's reflection will reveal that the only genuinely important moral imperatives relate to the well-being of conscious agents:

> Grounding our values in a continuum of conscious states – one that has the worst possible misery for everyone at its depths and differing degrees of well-being at all other points – seems like the only legitimate context in which to conceive of values and moral norms. Of course, anyone who has an alternative set of moral axioms is free to put them forward, just as they are free to define 'science' in any way they want. But some definitions will be useless, or worse – and many current definitions of 'morality' are so bad that we can know, far in advance of any breakthrough in the sciences of mind, that they have no place in any serious conversation about how we should live in this world.[12]

A modest version of Harris' claim here seems quite plausible, but rather banal – namely, that 'misery' is at one end of a moral spectrum and happiness and the development of human capacities at another. However, even once we have accepted that 'well-being' is valuable and 'misery' is evil (and have further accepted that there is some connection between 'well-being' and both physical pleasure and biological flourishing), we have hardly begun to scratch the surface of moral debate. A whole range of questions remain, questions which have preoccupied and perplexed secular philosophers as well as religious ones.

Disagreement with Harris will come, not on the value of 'well-being' and the evils of 'misery' but on the questions of (i) how in fact misery is to be minimised and well-being maximised, (ii) what well-being actually consists of, and (iii) whether the value of well-being and the disvalue of misery are the only moral values. Why, for example, should we assume that the only morally significant value is the impact of actions on our conscious states of experience? Harris offers the following argument:

> Without potential consequences at the level of experience … all talk of value is empty. Therefore, to say that an act is morally necessary, or evil, or blameless, is to make (tacit) claims about its consequences in the lives of conscious creatures (whether actual or potential). I am unaware of any interesting exception to this rule.[13]

The atheist philosopher Robert Nozick developed a famous and devastating argument against taking conscious experience to be the sole moral value. He invited his readers to consider whether they would value a life in which all human beings were plugged into an 'experience machine' offering maximally pleasurable states of consciousness.[14] His view is that nearly every one of us would decline to be plugged into such a machine. In the experience of one of the authors of this essay, when that question has been put to audiences – both religious and secular – the unanimous response has confirmed Nozick's view.

The universally negative response to the offer of an 'experience machine' demonstrates that human beings value things other than positive conscious states. We do not simply want life to be a succession of maximally positive experiences. Human beings want their lives to be, in some wider sense, meaningful. It seems that we value being in authentic contact and fellowship with other people. We want to live lives that in some sense add value to the world around us, whether that is by exercising artistic and intellectual creativity, caring for other human beings, or undertaking work that is vocational rather than simply remunerative. This indeed seems to be the position of the Amsterdam Declaration, for it affirms both "artistic creativity and imagination" and "the transforming power of art."

As Harris' case for the moral value of well-being is based on an appeal to our most powerful intuitions, he cannot simply dismiss Nozick's appeal to an equally powerful and widely-shared intuition. Yet, if he accepts the validity of this thought-experiment, his entire argument is in jeopardy. What Nozick's thought-experiment suggests is that human beings have a concern for what is actually going on in the external world in a way that is not solely tied to what human beings experience and what goes on in their conscious lives. That is to say, they reject any moral theory that locates value entirely in conscious experience.

Harris' other central claim is that the moral value of actions lies solely in their consequences. Again, most people's moral intuitions can be shown to run against Harris' position. A great deal of moral deliberation concerns situations where overall well-being may be enhanced by a course of action from which we nonetheless see as intrinsically wrong. Most of us do not take the ends to justify the means – hence, for example, the resistance to the use of torture in counter-terrorism operations. Many would disapprove of all torture of human beings, and an even greater number would reject outright the idea of torturing someone who is known to be innocent.

Harris might object that the wrongness of these acts still lies in their negative consequences for specific conscious agents. But being a 'consequentialist' involves far more than weighing acts in terms of their consequences for human agents. It involves the willingness to aggregate well-being. This leaves the consequentialist unable to rule out any way of treating other human beings. Given sufficiently large collective benefits, any amount of harm can be justified – a consequence Harris is all too willing to accept.

Harris is explicitly committed to aggregating well-being in exactly this way. In a revealing footnote, he considers another thought-experiment of Robert Nozick's. This concerns the possibility of "utility monsters" who gain such enormous satisfaction from devouring human beings that this outweighs the satisfaction lost in those prematurely ended human lives.[15] Harris wonders: Would it be ethical for our species to be "sacrificed for the unimaginably vast happiness of some superbeings"? His response is characteristically blunt: "Provided that we take the time to really imagine the details (which is not easy), I think the answer is clearly 'yes'."[16] Harris is sanguine about the implications of this answer. After all, he observes, it's just a story. "There is no compelling reason to believe that such superbeings exist, much less ones that want to eat us."[17]

In fact, Harris' response is far more revealing – and damaging – than he seems to imagine. Philosophers such as Nozick are not simply playing games when they present their outlandish thought-experiments. Such thought-experiments are designed to tease out what we take to be of fundamental value and why. And Harris' response to this thought-experiment is, in fact, rather chilling. It reveals that, for him, human beings have no specific and intrinsic dignity. If there is sufficient utility to be gained from their destruction and consumption, then we can imagine situations where that would be perfectly acceptable.

Harris has in fact been quite explicit about this elsewhere, and has argued that "if there is even one chance in a million that [the terrorist] will tell us something under torture that will lead to the further dismantling of Al Qaeda, it seems that we should use every means at our disposal to get him talking", and elsewhere that a pre-emptive nuclear strike on a weaponised Islamic state "may be the only course of action available to us." Given enough benefit to others, the large-scale murder of innocent civilians and the torture of suspected terrorists are, for this atheist "humanist" at least, morally imaginable.[18]

Harris' consequentialism undercuts any conception of humans as bearers of inalienable dignity or inviolable rights. His "humanism" really does turn out to cut off the branch it is sitting on – for what started off as a celebration of the dignity of the human (against the belittling fantasies of religion) is now willing to subject human beings to whatever trade-offs will maximise total wellbeing. Ironically, Harris turns out to be guilty of precisely the vices he attributes to the religious – he would allow the interests of a "superbeing" to override those of human beings. All that divides Harris from the jihadists he attacks is the factual question of whether such a being exists.

By contrast, Christian humanism regards the benevolence of God as every bit as intrinsic to his being as his omnipotence, and therefore *in principle* rules out this disregard for the dignity of each individual human being. While there are undoubtedly Christians who are not humanists (including some who advocate torture and pre-emptive nuclear strikes), all leading global Christian figures, such as Rowan Williams, John Paul II, Pope Benedict XVI, and Pope Francis, have offered a clear and high-profile critique of these dehumanising trade-offs of one life against another.

Harris claimed that one of the advantages of consequentialism was that it "correspond[s] to many of our intuitions about how the world works." We can now see that this is manifestly wrong. In reality, it takes a couple of our core moral intuitions (namely, that states of consciousness matter and that the moral significance of actions depends in a significant part on their consequences), and uses them to ride roughshod over other, equally central intuitions. There is no rational basis for doing this. Harris supplies no arguments for trusting the moral intuitions to which he appeals any more than the moral intuitions (about the intrinsic and inviolable dignity of each human being) which he completely ignores. As we have seen, a considerable part of his argument relies on eliding very plausible claims (namely, that conscious states and consequences are of huge moral significance) with much more extreme positions which do not follow from them, namely that nothing other than the production of positive conscious states is of value, and that there are no side constraints on what can be justified to promote such states.

If moral judgment were as closely tied to scientific knowledge as Harris suggests, it would not be hard to explain why our moral faculties track the truth – for we already have an explanation for the way our capacities for theoretical reasoning track the truth, and (on Harris' account) moral reasoning is more or less a subset of empirical science - once we have accepted the (non-empirical) premise that maximising aggregate pleasure and minimising aggregate pain are the only two moral imperatives. If, however, moral reasoning is a more complex and distinctive subject-matter, it becomes very difficult to explain how human beings have developed the distinct cognitive capacities that enable them to discern moral truths.

If we want to remain moral realists, the question arises of how we make the right choices in developing a moral code that goes beyond the imperatives of gene-, organism-, or species-replication. Richard Dawkins seeks to answer this question in *The God Delusion*. Dawkins suggests that we can "pull ourselves up by our bootstraps" now that humans have developed to a stage where we can reflect on the biological imperatives we have inherited. We can choose to act in ways that protect the weak and vulnerable, and to create communities which are not governed purely by the survival of the fittest.[19]

> There is going to be no evolutionary explanation available for that part of our moral cognition which does not maximise the survival and replication of the species.

This seems an accurate account of what goes on when we reason morally, but it fails to explain how we have the capacity for accurate moral reasoning. When we seek to 'pull ourselves up by our bootstraps', we take ourselves to have the capacity to discern what is morally better or worse. Natural selection can offer no account of why our moral intuitions and sentiments (insofar as they take us beyond the bare imperatives of survival and replication) should track an objective truth. There is going to be no evolutionary explanation available for that part of our moral cognition which does not maximise the survival and replication of the species. Yet, by Dawkins' own reckoning, it is that part of our moral cognition that enables us to make the most important ethical advances – to compassion and care for the weak.

# 5.

If Harris' and Dawkins' arguments seem problematic, are there any alternative positions atheist humanists might take? In the last few decades, atheist philosophers have used a great deal of energy to reconcile two apparently irreconcilable impulses. They want to reconcile the impulse towards *realism* in ethics (because moral truth does not simply change as our feelings and opinions change) with the equal and opposite impulse to *anti-realism* (because it is hard to explain how humans would evolve to know objective moral truths in an otherwise purposeless universe).

In this section, we will offer a more detailed critique of one such position, that of Simon Blackburn. We have chosen him because he is a prominent atheist humanist, and because we take his position to be the most credible (if ultimately unsuccessful) attempt to reconcile the appeal of realism and anti-realism. Inevitably, this takes us into some deep philosophical waters.[20]

Blackburn seeks to address the worry that, if ethics just expresses human attitudes – with no external standard of truth or falsehood – then anything would become morally acceptable if our attitudes changed. Blackburn accepts there is a legitimate worry here. We can't possibly accept any moral philosophy that says, "if we all approved of torturing people, then it would be ok."

If we root morality in our sentiments, how do we avoid that conclusion? Blackburn's answer is that morality is rooted in our actual sentiments, not in ones we might have had in another possible world. When we ask what would be (morally speaking) true if we had different commitments, the only sensible answer concerns what we (now, with our current commitments) make of the imagined situation. So, if we imagine human beings approving of torture, we will of course abhor what we are imagining. We might say: "If people in Britain began to approve of that, we would be a dreadful country!" And that – so Blackburn argues – is all we need to make sense of morality. On his account, moral truths do not "correspond to an objective order of reason," they simply represent what the most decent, sensitive and thoughtful human beings come to believe. (Blackburn calls this "quasi-realism.")

This view is superficially attractive – as it promises atheist humanists all the advantages of moral realism (the sense that it is somehow binding on us, and not something we make up as we go along) without the disadvantages – for the difficulty of explaining why human beings manage to 'track the truth' disappears on Blackburn's account.

The central problem with Blackburn's account comes when we consider how our moral convictions might change in the future. The openness human beings have to the correction of their moral attitudes extends further than a concern for the opinions and plans of our contemporaries. It is not merely that we are committed to allowing our views to be corrected by the current opinions of other human beings. We are open to the possibility of revisions in our communal moral outlook which go beyond making them more and more consistent. In principle, we admit that we could come to recognize that the prevailing consensus is wrong, and in consequence support more radical changes.

Consider how moral beliefs have changed in the last two centuries, on issues such as inter-racial marriage and the appropriate roles of men and women in public life. People's moral attitudes have changed in ways that are quite radical – it has been more than a matter of making them more intellectually consistent. If we asked Victorians to imagine a Britain in which the Prime Minister was female, they might well have said "If people in Britain began to approve of that, we would be a dreadful country!" But we today want to say that the Victorians were wrong and we are right. In addition, though, we also want to acknowledge that we may have our own blind-spots. Perhaps we have other prejudices that still need to be uncovered. Perhaps we will all come to think one day that killing and eating animals is barbaric – and future Britons will look back in amazement on the fact that this was legal in the twenty-first century.

The question of how our beliefs might change in the future places Blackburn in real difficulties.[21] On the one hand, he could say that we should judge our future selves simply by the attitudes we have today. But that ties morality too closely to our current beliefs: and paradoxically fails to recognise that "our current beliefs" are a bit less smug, and a bit more humble, than that. Today, most of us would acknowledge that – just as there have been some significant moral shifts since Victorian times – there may need to be more significant shifts in the future.

On the other hand, of course, Blackburn could accept that moral "quasi-truth" isn't tied to whatever we believe now – but accept that if our sentiments change, this kind of "truth" also changes. But then he is open to the very objection that he wanted to avoid, and it looks as if whatever we come to believe is (in this sense) "true".

So it seems that all those who say that moral "truth" is constructed out of human sentiments face an impossible dilemma. Either they have to say that moral "truth" is tied to the opinions of human beings in 2014, ruling out the possibility of any more of the emancipatory moral changes that have happened over the last two centuries happening over the next two. That seems dangerous: we cannot be that sure that we have no more moral blind-spots. Or they have to say that moral truth develops as our sentiments change and develop. But that too seems dangerous: for we do not want to say that if (like the Nazis in Germany) we began to think torturing the innocent was acceptable, then it would indeed be ok. The only way to avoid these dilemmas is to accept that moral truth is in fact objective – to make the same move the atheist philosopher Philippa Foot made back in 1945:

> It was significant that when I came back to Oxford in 1945, that was the time when the news of the concentration camps was coming out. This news was shattering in a fashion that no one now can easily understand ... [I]n the face of the news of the concentration camps, I thought 'it just can't be ... that morality in the end is just the expression of an attitude.' ... For, fundamentally, there is no way, if one takes this line, that one could imagine oneself saying to a Nazi, 'but we are right, and you are wrong' with there being any substance to the statement.[22]

Accepting Foot's argument, and rejecting attempts to water down moral realism, saves atheist humanism from one dilemma. But it does so at a heavy cost. As we saw in our discussions of Sam Harris and Richard Dawkins, atheists find it very difficult to explain how humans come to knowledge of objective moral truths.

The British Humanist Association acknowledges that, philosophically, atheist humanism is a broad church. Its Humanist Philosophers' Group, which includes Simon Blackburn, has written a pamphlet which explores the breadth and limits of (atheistic) humanism.[23] While commenting negatively on 'Platonic realism' (which it defines as the view that goodness and justice would exist even if there were no conscious beings at all), the BHA Philosophers' Group writes that

> there remains a philosophical debate between what are called 'realist' and 'anti-realist' views about values... There is no humanist orthodoxy on these difficult questions. Nevertheless we think that just as humanism should distance itself from a 'divine command' theory of morality or a Platonic realism, so it should also distance itself from what we shall call 'crude subjectivism' and 'crude relativism'.[24]

What we have sought to do in this chapter is engage at some depth with a spectrum of atheist humanist views. Our aim has been to show that, *whichever* brand of atheist humanism is preferred its account of ethical value is deeply problematic.

## 6.

We began this chapter by considering the Amsterdam Declaration, and its commitment to humanism as "ethical." We have considered just what kind of subject-matter ethics actually is. In particular, are moral truths constructed out of human sentiments, or do our sentiments point us to something genuinely objective – something beyond our opinions and cultural norms, which those opinions and norms are trying to get right?

Our conclusion has been twofold. Firstly, we have argued that atheistic humanism has real trouble explaining why human reason and empathy should be a guide to any kind of objective moral truth. We have contrasted that the account Christian humanists give of the nature of morality, and of human knowledge of it.

Secondly, we have argued that there are even greater difficulties if humanists abandon their belief in moral realism. We have explained why the accounts of non-realists such as Simon Blackburn fail to do justice to the inviolable dignity of human beings, a dignity which does not wax and wane with changes in our opinions and sentiments. Humanism, we suggest, is most naturally combined with moral realism – for only moral realism gives a robust enough account of the dignity of every human being, while also allowing for the possibility of truly emancipatory moral change.

Christianity, we have suggested throughout this essay, has the capacity to resolve some of these difficulties in humanism, and to develop a narrative which does justice to the innate dignity of human beings. That this may seem a surprising conclusion is in part our own fault, for Christians have sometimes allowed a picture to develop on which ethics is just the arbitrary legislation of an all-powerful being, who is to be obeyed simply because of his capacity to punish and reward us. Whoever's fault these misunderstandings are, we need to recognise that picture as a mere parody, for it bears little relation to the central Christian conviction that humanity is created and redeemed by God at great cost. The central doctrines of Christianity – of a God who is love, a human race created in his image, and the sacrifice of Jesus Christ – provide a durable foundation for the ethics which all humanists cherish.

# chapter 4 – references

1. Entry on "Ethics" in Robert Audi (ed), *Cambridge Dictionary of Philosophy* (Cambridge UP, 1995).
2. St Augustine, *Confessions*, Chapter 1.
3. 1 John 4.19.
4. Pope Benedict XVI, Deus Caritas Est (online at http://www.vatican.va/holy_father/benedict_xvi/encyclicals/documents/hf_ben-xvi_enc_20051225_deus-caritas-est_en.html), §18.
5. *What is humanism?* (BHA Philosophers Group, 2002), pp. 15ff.
6. In *From Morality to Metaphysics*, Angus Ritchie defines moral realism, as belief in the following theses:

    (1) The moral order has certain properties, independently of either human beliefs or conceptual schemes. Indeed, the moral order would exist and have properties even if no human beings existed at all; and

    (2) A moral judgement is true if and only if it is an adequate representation of the way the moral order is, where 'the world' is as construed in (1).

    Angus Ritchie, *From Morality to Metaphysics: The Theistic Implications of our Moral Commitments* (Oxford University Press, 2012), p. 40.
7. Sam Harris, *The Moral Landscape: How Science can determine Human Values* (Black Swan, 2012), p. 43.
8. Harris, *Moral Landscape*, p. 44. Italics in orginal text.
9. A.C. Grayling, *What is good? Searching for the best way to live* (London: Phoenix, 2003).
10. Grayling, *The Choice of Hercules*.
11. This is a question Angus Ritchie has pressed against atheist worldviews in his book *From Morality to Metaphysics*, and the accompanying Theos report *From Goodness to God: why religion makes sense of our moral commitments*. We can only offer a summary of those arguments here, but readers who want to explore them in greater depth can refer to those more extended statements of the position.
12. Harris, *Moral Landscape*, p. 61.
13. Harris, *Moral Landscape*, pp. 85-6.
14. Robert Nozick, *Anarchy, state, and utopia*. (New York: Basic Books, 1974), pp. 42-45.
15. Nozick, *Anarchy*, p. 14.
16. Harris, *Moral Landscape*, p. 271.
17. Harris, *Moral Landscape*, p. 271.
18. Harris, *The End of Faith: Religion, Terror and the Future of Reason* (Free Press, 2006), pp. 198 and 129.
19. Dawkins, *God Delusion*, p. 222.

20  A much fuller critique of Blackburn's position – and of a range of other secular philosophers who attempt the same task in different ways – is offered by Angus Ritchie's book *From Morality to Metaphysics*. Our discussion of Blackburn is based on his statement of his position in 'Errors and the Phenomenology of Value', in his *Essays in Quasi-realism* (Oxford: Oxford University Press, 1993), pp. 152–3 and *Ruling Passions* (Oxford: Oxford University Press, 1998).

21  Blackburn's position is the main focus of Chapter 3 of *From Morality to Metaphysics*.

22  Alex Voorhoeve, 'The Grammar of Goodness: An Interview with Philippa Foot', *Harvard Review of Philosophy* 11 (2003), pp. 33-34.

23  *What is humanism?* sadly does not leave room for Christian humanism, although it acknowledges legitimate usages of the word which do – see p. 4.

24  *What is humanism?* pp. 12-13.